The Ever-Transcending Quest

1. Sri Chinmoy's blessingful smile, circa 1997

The Ever-Transcending Quest

A Literary Analysis of the Poetry of Sri Chinmoy

Mrinali C. Clarke

With a Foreword by
Purushottama Bilimoria

DK PRINTWORLD
Publishers of Indian Traditions

Cataloging in Publication Data — DK
[Courtesy: D.K. Agencies (P) Ltd. <docinfo@dkagencies.com>]

Clarke, Mrinali C., 1952-

The ever-transcending quest : a literary analysis of the poetry of Sri Chinmoy / Mrinali C. Clarke ; with a foreword by Purushottama Bilimoria.

p. cm.

Includes bibliographical references (p.) and index.

ISBN : 9788124608029

1. Chinmoy, Sri, 1931-2007 – Criticism and interpretation. I. Title.

DDC 823.91409 23

ISBN 13: 978-81-246-0802-9

First published in India in 2015

Printed and published by:
D.K. Printworld (P) Ltd.
Regd. Office : *Vedaśrī*, F-395, Sudarshan Park
(Metro Station: Ramesh Nagar)
New Delhi – 110 015.
Phones : (011) 2545 3975, 2546 6019; *Fax* : 2546 5926
E-mail : indology@dkprintworld.com
Web : www.dkprintworld.com

To my Master,

Sri Chinmoy Kumar Ghose,

who spent the second half of his life based in New York City,
teaching the Western world about spirituality,
and who chose me as one of his disciples.
For this I am deeply, eternally grateful,
for it saved me and shaped my life
into a more joyful, fulfilling and
purposeful experience.

Foreword

IT GIVES ME great pleasure to pen this short foreword to the literary analysis of the poetry of Sri Chinmoy by Mrinali Clarke. This study is quite a tour de force. Few would know what an accomplished and prolific poet in his own right Sri Chinmoy was, if he is much known at all outside of certain circles of meditation.

Over the years I have dipped into the poems of Sri Chinmoy that have graced my bookshelves; these works came to me from a number of sources, from students and friends who have had close associations with Sri Chinmoy such as Kishore Cunningham, who for decades has directed the Sri Chinmoy Centre in Melbourne, Australia, and Dr Vidagdha Bennett, who I came to know through her Ph.D. thesis on Sri Chinmoy's literary work that (completed at The University of Melbourne, and cited in this work).

I had the rare privilege also of attending a public event some two decades back in Melbourne when Sri Chinmoy visited Australia, and regaled a full house in a theatre-hall with his melodious singing and recitation of poems from his prolific output. I gained a favourable impression of an adept dedicated to spreading the message of peace and love to the world.

I was also aware that Sri Chinmoy introduced meditation

sessions and ran regular meetings at the United Nations assembly. Indeed, the peace Initiatives that he engaged in through the many years he lived in New York and travelled throughout the world, register a legendary contribution, alongside the dedicated work of Sri Aurobindo, Gandhi, H. H. Dalai Lama, Nelson Mandela and Martin Luther King Jr.

Further, there was another side to Sri Chinmoy that also always intrigued me and that was his connection with music, and teaching that music had the capacity to uplift and change consciousness. It was common knowledge during my university years that Sri Chinmoy had some considerable influence on two of my favourite modern instrumentalist musicians, Santana and John McLachlan (of the Maha Vishnu Orchestra); in fact, I still have in my possession, a cherished vinyl LP of these two collaborators on an album called "Love, Devotion and Surrender", the back cover with a photograph of the two maestros of modern guitar either side of Sri Chinmoy.

Apart from that, I would consider myself a novice and a dilettante when it comes to the plethora of the immensely rich collection of poems and amazing other literary productions that Sri Chinmoy has bequeathed to the world. Hungry to learn more about how Sri Chinmoy composed his poems, what literary traditions he drew from, and where did the roots of this poetical compositions could be said to be found, I welcomed, the opportunity to read Mrinali's work, and encouraged her to publish and further expand her output towards journal articles.

I have come to appreciate, as I hope the readers of this study will also do, the gift that Sri Chinmoy seemed to possess in composing rather pithy, short poems that are more playful than they are technical unlike some of the modern poems our secular times tend to be. One is reminded here of the short *shloka* forms in Sanskrit *kavya* (poetry), in *alamkaras* (aesthetic evocations), as well as *mantra*-chants and lyrics from devotional compositions of savants such as Kabir, Mirabai, Surdas, Tulsidas, Tukarm, and, closer to our times, Sri Aurobindo (in his magnum poetical work *Savitri*). Mrinali alludes to the metaphysical and transcendental poets from Western traditions, specifically the works of Whitman, Emerson, and Dickenson.

Common sense or what Indian philosophers call *laukika-jnana (para-vidya)* is questioned for its boastful claims and shown to be demonstrably lacking in what lies beyond its understanding and reaches, both within and without. But what is equally more enticing and seductive, I might say, about Sri Chinmoy's poems, is the style he has evolved, in particular his own unique use of compound nouns playing the role of gerundives and simple adjectives that are able to do the work of an entire phrase, and strategically "hit-the-spot" moving the reader quickly to the next line that, in a short few words, brings the poem to its crescendo. In this context, the haiku comes also to mind. No complex hermeneutical devices have to be provided to get to the sense and the particular nuance intended; the meaning as it were flows out directly in the very first reading: the word is the *meaning*. I wish to give an example of what I might suggest is my favourite that speaks to the philosophic style and innovative literalism that Mrinali analyses and gives expression to in her study:

In the Universal Heart

In the universal heart all hearts are one,
    inseparable, I know.
Yet knowing this I hurt the hearts of others
    day and night.
We are all the slaves of fate;
It dances on our foreheads.
In peace sublime is the extinction-sleep of fate.
I know this secret.
O Jewel of my eye, pour into my heart
    Your golden Silence.

In this beautiful piece we can feel the individual moving through the mired snares of worldly knowledge towards the golden silence that hides ultimately in the heart.

In the pages that follow, I invite the reader to enjoy the selection of poems that Mrinali has chosen for her study and commentary – a drop in the ocean of the vast work that Sri Chinmoy seems to have so devotedly produced, which could fill the pages of an epic such as the southern rendition of the *Ramayana.* One would equally be enlightened by the added literary and textual wisdom that she analytically brings to the lively poetic adventure – from this amazing savant of the *yoga* of life – spanning literature, music, art and inner peace through sports. This calls for celebration and a timely recognition, more widely beyond academic halls or societies of secret poets, of the world-sustaining contribution that Sri Chinmoy has made.

Venus Bay, Australia **Purushottama Bilimoria**
July 2014

Contents

Acknowledgement

I AM GREATLY indebted to Dr Vidagdha Bennett for her extensive scholarship and extraordinary insight into the writings and life of Sri Chinmoy, as well as for her encouragement and unstinting efforts in reading and offering guidance and advice, editing, and coaching as I updated this work!

I would also like to thank both Animesh Harrington for his generous advice and input, and Prachar Stegemann for his reading and correction of many details in the short biographical sketch of Sri Chinmoy.

Finally my gratitude goes to Purushottama Bilimoria for encouraging me to continue to write articles on the literature of Sri Chinmoy, and to publish this work, a work that was initially written in the 1980s.

Introduction

It is hard to hear a new voice, as hard as it is to listen to an unknown language. . . . Why? – Out of fear. The world fears a new experience more than it fears anything . . .?

– D.H. Lawrence[1]

You do not dare to know
The real truth.
He does not dare to face
The real light.
I do not dare to attain
The real silence.
– Sri Chinmoy[2]

Does our own age fear a new spiritual voice? Lawrence was talking of a new voice to be found in the early American classics, while Sri Chinmoy's poem here indicates that same instinctive aversion in relation to the new spiritual experience. How relevant then are Lawrence's comments in relation to the poetry of Sri Chinmoy at the end of the twentieth century and the beginning of a new millennium?

---

1 *Studies in Classic American Literature.*

2 *Surrender Rose Blossoms*, song #42.

A common criticism of metaphysical poetry is that it is only understood by the initiated. If the poetry of Sri Chinmoy is placed in that category then it may also be restricted by traditional standards and expectations of the genre. Traditionally, literary evaluations tend to concentrate on poetic complexity or multiplicity in a way that masks or fails to uncover what really may be a distinctively new voice of the age, particularly in this case in relation to spiritual poetry. Sri Chinmoy has intimated that the reading of his poetry and prose can be utilized as a method of entering into a higher state of consciousness for the novice, the seeker or the reader; in effect, a method of contacting or awakening the reader's own inner pathway into this higher, more universal plane of consciousness.[3] This in itself is a revolutionary innovation.

The idea of a poetic voice expressing or evoking pure consciousness is, of course, a paradoxical problem, for it raises the conundrum – how can one express in mere words an experience of such a subjective metaphysical nature, or, in other words, how does one "express the inexpressible"? The daunting nature of such a task has, however, never discouraged the artist or writer from attempting it. If we witness the poetic stance of

[3] *The Summits of God-Life: Samadhi and Siddhi.* This is a brief outline of Sri Chinmoy's definition: Consciousness is the inner spark, the golden link within that connects our highest and most illumined part with our lowest. It is the connecting link between Heaven and Earth. Heaven is in our consciousness. Consciousness houses silence and it houses power. Consciousness and the soul can never be separated, whereas the body can easily be separated from consciousness (pp. 1ff).

George Herbert, John Donne, William Wordsworth, Walt Whitman, Gerald Manley Hopkins and Emily Dickinson, they are all in some degree attempting to relay their own experience of the relationships between the body and spirit, time and eternity, matter and consciousness; and to explore the most complex and intricate secrets of the essence of existence. They each devised a tailored style and form arising out of their own unique needs and perceptions. Sri Chinmoy also has endeavoured to forge a new style and a new language to express the particular vision of his transcendental experiences.

Sri Chinmoy came to the US in 1964 with the express inner compulsion to offer the fruits of his own realisation to the Western world. His philosophy emphasizes a kind of marriage between Western dynamism and Eastern spirituality – a path which promotes self-transcendence through the inner peace of the heart.[4] In his attraction to the dynamic nature of Western culture, Sri Chinmoy leaves behind the spiritual views of the past whereby one must practise meditation alone and shut off from the world.[5] I will argue that the spirit of the poetry of Sri Chinmoy is a natural progression from, and an extension of, the American Transcendentalist tradition, and I will concentrate on making any points of comparison with poets that I view in this context.

Sri Chinmoy's poetic language is highly distinctive in comparison to many other styles, particularly in devotional poetry.

---

[4] Biographical notes on Sri Chinmoy.

[5] For example, Sri Chinmoy is founding director of Sri Chinmoy: The Peace Meditation at the United Nations.

It denotes a rather more innocent approach, rather than sophistication; not so much building on past traditions but taking universal themes and starting afresh. His use of the most basic, and simple language and tropes, brief lyrics, even aphoristic or haiku-styled poems, allows for the portrayal of very intimate but singularly significant moments in the spiritual journey of an individual. These moments then often tend to indicate a larger and more unified context of spirituality – the vision he holds of the absolute oneness of the universe. The personal and the universal are always present in each other.[6]

In this introduction I shall discuss this very characteristic feature of Sri Chinmoy's poetry: the distilling down to a specific concept, which in contemplation then expands the awareness into the inferred reality beyond the physical world. I shall also look at the simple style and language used by Sri Chinmoy to see in what manner and to what extent they reflect the message he wishes to convey. Furthermore, I shall outline the criteria for the particular poems chosen for the study from the prolific poetic works available, indicating why I think they are representative and centrally related to the wider vision of Sri Chinmoy's transcendentalist teaching.

For the most part, the poetic language of Sri Chinmoy is stripped bare of intricate nature imagery, or complex and

---

[6] For a more extensive comparison of Sri Chinmoy's poetry in relation to the traditions of spiritual poetry, as well as the influences of his native Bengali traditions, reference must be made to the 1981 Doctoral Thesis at the University of Melbourne by Dr Vidagdha Meredith Bennett, *Simplicity and Power: The Poetry of Sri Chinmoy 1971-1981*, New York: Aum Publications, 1992.

extended metaphorical tropes. Additionally, the poet uses traditional forms of rhyme and metre quite sparingly, preferring instead the contained brevity of the lyric form in the style of free verse. However, Sri Chinmoy does use the more common metrical forms and rhyme schemes for certain vital themes, as I will show in Chapter 3. In any case, he never fails to maintain his brevity of style and, coupled with the subject matter of the spiritual path, this adds to the heightened austerity of the tone. As Alan Spence has indicated, there are very few things of a material or concrete description in the poetry of Sri Chinmoy, and those things which are to be found, are used as an archetypal code, a symbolic language of man's inner spiritual life.[7]

> . . . O Bird of Light, O Bird of Light,
> With Your glowing and flowing flames
> Do enter into my heart once again . . .[8]

The "Bird of Light" is often used by the poet to describe both the divine human soul, as well as the aspiration, feeling of glowing elation, or uplifting movement in the heart during meditation, attributed to the connection with the soul's light.

> The golden Boat
> Is beauty's speed.
> The golden Shore
> Is divinity's crown.
> The golden Dream,
> Reality dreams.

---

[7] Alan Spence (ed.), *Introduction Between Nothingness & Eternity, poems by Sri Chinmoy*, p. 9.

[8] Sri Chinmoy, *The Garden of Love Light*, p. 43.

The golden Pilot,
Eternity claims.[9]

Similarly, here Sri Chinmoy extends the common trope of the sea of life, to illustrate his chosen path to God as the Boat, the Shore as the goal of realisation, the Dream as God's vision for humanity, and the Pilot as God Himself, both inner and outer aspects.

I would like to argue that this paring down or reductive tendency, the very simplicity of language, is one of the quintessential ingredients of Sri Chinmoy's poetry, as it mimics the message he is attempting to convey – that of the surprisingly simple but profound nature of consciousness itself. To express the transcendental consciousness, Sri Chinmoy must illustrate feelings of "soulfulness", a task he attempts as though it were as easy and as natural as the expression of joy, love, honour and so on. The simplicity, purity and power of the poet's language are facilitated by such methods as the Sanskrit *mantra* and *sutra*, which he brings to his poetic style in English from his native Bengali traditions.[10]

---

[9] Sri Chinmoy, *Selections from the Golden Boat*, p. 1.

[10] Alan Spence briefly outlines these techniques: "A *mantra* is in its simplest form a syllable or set of syllables, chanted aloud as an aid to meditation. There is an awareness here of the power of the word as incantation, invocation. Poetry described as mantric actually invokes the qualities it describes." And *sutra* "Literally it means thread, and it is used to describe series of terse, aphoristic utterances. . . . These offer instruction in the path of *yoga*, and are tight, densely packed, designed to be memorised and recited aloud, gradually unfolding their truth." Op. cit., p. 8.

There is a necessity then for this style of expression to be freed from extraneous connotations of worldly associations and experience, and the intellectual transactions of the mental faculties. It must be recognized that this is where the traditional schools of poetic expression diverge from the voice which Sri Chinmoy chooses. His choice is not to rely on the imaginative faculty of the mind, but to utilize and merge with the more intuitive and instinctive connections of the soul with the Highest Consciousness, producing, in many instances, poems which are created whole rather than "worked out" or developed in the usual fashion of drafting over and again. This complicates and frustrates the role of the literary critic, whose tools of analysis tend to involve the intellect as the mainstay, and any higher creative functions, such as intuition, as merely an inspirational bonus. In addition, it raises the question of what category of literature we are dealing with here, and what possible evaluations we *can* make of the poetry.

The experience of the poetry of Sri Chinmoy illustrates that the Absolute Highest Consciousness of the divine can be more easily apprehended by the heart: a psychic centre of the being, which is closest to the soul and, therefore, according to this *yogi's* teaching, manifests similar qualities such as purity, delight and humility. The faculty of the heart is separate from the faculty of the mind, whose step by step, analytical and critical functions tend to interfere and distract, reducing all ideas to a discursive or dialectical level (a problematical situation which is well known to individuals practising meditation). Therefore, descriptive density as such would be counter-productive and superfluous in this case since it would tend to engage the imaginative intellect rather than the heart. What the poet is trying to achieve is a purity and simplicity of expression, which take on a most particular significance and beauty – in a way, elevating the language. In addition, if it is correct that the consciousness of the heart can directly apprehend or intuit as it were some kind of spiritual truth or experience, then this certainly has some interesting implications in the argument about whether language is used to express reality or whether reality can be shaped by language.

Sri Chinmoy explains this further dimension of communication:

> The soul uses the soul's language, which is light. It is through light that the soul expresses itself. When the soul's light expresses itself to the physical in us, the physical mind gets the message in a way it can understand. It is not actually words that the soul is using. The soul is offering and scattering its light and the physical is receiving it in the way that it finds most convincing.[11]

In other words, what we would call a "flash of intuition" can occur; or perhaps it can be recognized as that some time familiar "twinge of conscience". One technique that Sri Chinmoy uses to express or illustrate this "flash" or message from the consciousness of the soul is the compound noun, an interesting feature of his style because of its unique nature. Bennett hails Sri Chinmoy's use of the compound noun as a new form, working for a conceptual advance ". . . used to indicate a development in man's comprehension of God",[12] and makes

---

[11] Sri Chinmoy, *Light of the Beyond*, p. 41.

[12] Bennett, op. cit., pp. 40ff.

extensive comparisons of the use of this feature by other poets.

The compound noun can in fact be seen as an emblem of the unity of the form and the message. Rather than being vague or indefinite, it can produce that unique precision and compactness which at once comes down to a single image and then expands into the vision of the universal reality of being; for example: "welkin-rim", the slightly curved, outer edge of the firmament, upper sky or heavens, beyond land to the unknown; "nectar-silence", sweet, fluid, nourishing substance not absence, food of the gods; and, "Father–Son", with its Christ allusions, the state of realisation, the lover and the beloved become interchangeable.

The brevity of Sri Chinmoy's poems in no way detracts from the qualities of concentration and intensity of the poetic image, rather the effort in reading helps one to the intuited feeling of a truth revealed. A leap of imagination is not needed here. Shakespeare in the same way seemed to bridge this gap, the communication of the deep mysteries of human life, with aphoristic utterances of universal significance, which have since passed into the common colloquialism. For example, *Hamlet* comes easily to mind: "What a piece of work is man . . ." and "To be or not to be: That is the question. . . ."

If then this seeming simplicity of language masks merely the subtlety of expression of a heightened consciousness of the poet, how may we read the poems correctly to apprehend this experience ourselves? Do we in fact recreate the experience of the poet as we read what he has written? Or is it a closed and very select fraternity of spiritual adepts who will gain entry into this experience of the highest? To explore these questions through the language of the poetry, I have chosen what I see as a particular group of related poems. These poems I have united under a single theme – the ancient topos of "the Quest". The spiritual quest for Self-Realisation or God-Realisation, which is a common theme in poetry of a transcendental nature, is predominant in even the most cursory glance through the writings of Sri Chinmoy. His prolific output can in fact be more easily apprehended as the united work of a lifetime in the light of the topos of *The Quest*. Whilst reading for a selection of poems under this guise it became clear to me that many poems were interrelated. Significant patterns of development and convergence seemed to form themselves. Keeping in mind Bennett's proposition that there can be no "measured sequence" imposed on the poetry of Sri Chinmoy[13], I nevertheless felt compelled to arrange them in the ascending pattern of complexity that follows.

Throughout the poetry of Sri Chinmoy I have discovered the three parts of a Quest – namely Separation, Trial and Return – become a more complex and integrated journey of life for the spiritual seeker to follow on the road to the highest Goal. To illustrate this complexity, I have further divided the poems into the following steps:

SEPARATION

1. Evolution of the soul
2. Oneness with the Absolute before incarnation
3. The Quest begins

---

[13] Bennett, op. cit., p. 249.

4. Loss of oneness
5. Descent into ignorance/loneliness

TRIAL

6. Trials of a seeker of the truth
7. Despair and loss of faith
8. Descent of God's Compassion
9. Nearing the Goal
10. Temptation

RETURN

11. Unconditional surrender
12. Attaining the Goal: God/Self-Realisation
13. Manifestation
14. And Beyond.[14]

Sri Chinmoy demonstrates the insights of a Self-Realised spiritual mystic and teacher in his very large collections (*Ten Thousand Flower-Flames*, *Twenty-Seven Thousand Aspiration-Plants*, both published in the early 1980s and *Seventy-Seven Thousand Service-Trees*, published during the 1990s). However, the poems chosen here are mainly taken from collections published in the early 1970s, many translated by the poet from his original Bengali, which are not as overtly instructional and display more conventional literary merits. My intention is to briefly explore the way Sri Chinmoy has re-defined and extended the normally

[14] The use of capitals is consistent with the poet's use to denote qualities pertaining to the Supreme Being.

accepted limits of the spiritual quest, especially in relation to three American poets, Whitman, Dickinson and Snyder, who can be seen to take up the thread of the American Transcendentalist tradition. This poet's prophetic voice represents a challenge to humanity, to re-examine our destiny in a new light. But as well it throws new light on the complete interdependence of the relationship between aspiring humanity and the self-transcending nature of the Supreme Being.

Through this brief survey of poetry we may glean some connections between the style of Sri Chinmoy's poetry and his wider purpose of presenting the Goal of the transcendental consciousness. I must emphasize however that the scope of this study represents no more than a minute foray into such a large body of poetic work, not all of which by any means can be so readily categorized by my own schema of the spiritual quest. The Quest arose as a natural choice of theme. It contained the study to a small and unified sample, which I have edited down into a kind of "reader's guide". This not only readily admitted the connections between the cryptic style of language, the surface simplicity and the complex and often paradoxical attitudes, but also would show some sense of the development and fulfilment of the transcendental vision as it unfolds from within the poet's own experience.

1

The Separation

IN THE INTRODUCTION I defined the Quest in general terms as a journey of life for the spiritual seeker towards the goal of God-Realisation. To further assist us in our understanding of this concept, it was divided into three parts – namely Separation, Trial and Return. In this chapter we explore the first part of the Quest, the theme of Separation, through the poetry of Sri Chinmoy using the following motifs which interweave and overlap throughout the writings.

Separation

- Evolution of the soul
- Oneness with the Absolute before incarnation
- The Quest begins
- Loss of oneness
- Descent into ignorance/loneliness

In looking at a selection of poetry by Sri Chinmoy, loosely grouped here under the heading of *Separation*, we first encounter poems that concentrate on the soul's evolution from the animal kingdom into the human world. In the teachings of Sri Chinmoy, it is not only the physical that evolves, but also the soul that is in evolution. The soul as a portion of the Supreme

Being manifests itself in the physical world. The inconscience of the dense physical plane then intervenes to blanket the soul's actual union with the Divine – the Oneness before birth is forgotten, the Quest then begins and so the "Divine Lila" or Cosmic Game plays itself out over millennia.[1]

The first two poems sweep back through past aeons of the evolution of the human consciousness from the animal, and so are pre-separation in theme. They attempt to infer a time that is prior to differentiated consciousness in a circular motion. First, the animal world is a world of unthinking, wild and instantaneous gratification with a rhythmical physiological impulse of organic life. They look back to that past as a time of great slumber, the sleep of unawakened consciousness. Nevertheless, they also look forward to a future, a time of the awakened divinity in humanity.

Pulse of the Past

O pulse of the past,
I do not need you
To found my reality on earth.
O pulse of the past,
My future dreams
Are growing fast
In my today's reality.
O pulse of the past,
My animal past
Was my destruction-night;

[1] Many of the books written by Sri Chinmoy are available from : http://www.srichinmoylibrary.com

My human past
Was my future dream;
My divine past
Has become one with the immediacy of today.[2]

This poem uses the simple format of repetition, with a softening alliteration; the pairing of "pulse" and "past" giving both a mantric quality and rhetorical tone, as well as affirming a rhythmic pace through the piece. The image of the pulse emphasizes this rhythmic march of evolution. It infers the scope of aeons, while the rhetorical tone imparts a ringing emphasis to the opening emphatic denial of any obligation or restrictions by previous realities. The second stanza softens and opens out the theme with the word 'dreams' and the rhyming of past/ fast. Past, present and future are linked as one continuum, but it is not until the last stanza that we understand in what manner.

The poem is dealing with an evolutionary scale of being – a vast canvass – and speaking from the consciousness of the eternally evolving soul. The animal past is acknowledged but cast off as a destructive phase, the compound noun evoking more a sense of the Dark Age of the soul. Surprisingly, the contrasting parallel is drawn with "my human past" as something already outgrown or outdated. This "future dream" indicates the paradoxical perspective of the mystic who sees from the highest perspective the aspiration of humanity to leave its restrictions behind for an ever more perfect vision. The odd syntactical formulations, however, point to the future dream as already being realised, the growth through the human phase,

---

[2] Sri Chinmoy, *Selections from The Golden Boat*, p. 43.

into the phase of the divine growth of the soul. The last two lines reveal a further parallel, prefiguring the endlessness of the evolutionary process after the realisation of the divine phase: the immediacy of today instigates new incentives. The movement of the poem from past to present and future imperatives offers the message of transcendence through the idea of evolution, an epic significance often surprising to discover in such short lyrics.

The Story of My Common Sense

When my common sense
Was fast asleep,
I lived in the animal kingdom.
I felt and filled my hungry abyss.
When I surrendered
My common sense to my Inner Pilot,
Peace-sea, sun-world, love-heaven
At long last
Discovered their permanence
In my God-hunger supreme.[3]

The poetic quality of this verse is simply manifested by the arrangement of lines, and the development of a musical quality by soft echoes and alliteration. Again, the progression of ideas from unconsciousness and more primitive satisfactions of the animal world to the permanence of the higher goal, the longing for the divine, illustrates the epic dimension of the individual soul's evolution. Here we witness the marriage of ideas in the

[3] Sri Chinmoy, *The Dance of Life*, vol. 1, p. 18.

compound noun, used to suggest qualities or experiences of the inner life and awakening consciousness. Any banality of the terms used is banished by the strength of the newly-formed conceptual imagery, particularly noticeable if the poem is read aloud. Enunciated clearly it slows the pace of the poem and creates an immediate experience like an invocation: the peace that permeates inwardly, the world illumined, and the heaven of a love free of human ties. Although childlike in their simplicity, these messages form the clarity of a deeper and purer vision, an inner existence that is at home in the meditative state of consciousness.

After looking back to the sleep of the unawakened consciousness, the poem explores the possibilities of the human, and sees that it is only when surrender comes to the awareness within, to the evolved soul, or what Sri Chinmoy calls the "Inner Pilot", that real self-consciousness is possible – and this is inextricably linked to the "God-hunger supreme". Mankind's relationship with the Supreme Being is never portrayed as subservient or manipulative, the discovery is of an inner yearning, an incompletion of the self, the natural progression of the appetite for God-knowledge, so that God is both the goal and the satisfaction of a need.

Two further characteristics prominent in the tone of the poetry of Sri Chinmoy are the profoundly authoritative nature that is evinced by prophetic statements and themes, set against the intimate mood of revelation or personal confidences given. This is evident in a further example of a poem touching on the evolutionary theme. What appears to be a childlike dramatization occurs because of the sonic simplicity of language and tone. Short words, brief and simple statements, and the use of anaphora, as well as the resonances of the Christ, all impart a kind of biblical reverberation.

Why Men Cry

I tell you in supreme secrecy,
God will become a man,
God will cry like a man.
God will become a man
To see what man needs most.
God will cry like a man
To see why men cry.[4]

The strength of the repetition and rhetorical accents is reinforced by the image played around God's Will. The poem is a poignant notation on the lack of knowledge between the two perspectives, the human and the divine, portrayed without moral tone, but presented in the light of God's boundless compassion, love and concern for humanity. It places this prophetic incarnation of the Supreme Consciousness in an empathetic rather than a judgemental context. The simplicity of the language masks an interesting intersection of truth and ignorance, need and fulfilment, intimacy and authority. The repetition serves to impart a reassuring tone in defiance of the modern propensity for alienation and scepticism from the divine.

Further background on the imperative for the quest can now be finely discerned in the following three poems:

---

[4] Sri Chinmoy, *When God Love Descends*, p. 42.

Unrecognized

Humanity is divinity
  Yet unrecognized.
Divinity is reality
  Yet unrecognized.
Reality is totality
  Yet unrecognized.[5]

This poem, presented in a triple-tiered epigrammatic form, displays a semantic and ideational symmetry. Sri Chinmoy commonly uses this form, which serves to give equal weight to each concept in the statement, while providing a hierarchy of ideas impossible to resist. The equal number of syllables in each rhyming pair, and the intensifying prophetic interjection emphasizes the weight of each philosophic deliberation. Again, the childlike neatness of the equations evokes that transparent simplification and clarity of thought which defies the grandeur of the conceptual analysis – an analysis which almost threatens to slip out of cognitive reach at the last, as one slides through the hierarchical scale of definitions. The rhetorical tone at the close adds to the quite solemn coercion toward this universal view.

This kind of ambiguity, or merging of identity, occurs also in the following, which illustrates the interdependency of the quest for both the human and the divine fulfilment.

My Heart Became God

My heart became God
  Out of pure necessity.

[5] Sri Chinmoy, *Lord, Receive This Little Undying Cry*, p. 44.

My mind became man
Out of sheer curiosity.[6]

The simplicity of the statements and the parallel images defies the complex paradox of God-becoming and man-incarnating as one entity. The image of the heart paired with God, and its motivation "pure necessity", suggest God's own reliance on human progress, while the mind, paired with man, and the equally weighed motivation "sheer curiosity" emphasize the inherent human quality, as well as completing the dizzying circular movement of the soul's evolution in one form. We are compelled to identify with this speaker, from perhaps an even higher perspective than both man and God – from the imperative of evolution itself.

This brief glance at some background ideas in the poet's work gives some understanding of how his vision reconciles these notions of creation and evolution. Having some understanding of this, it is interesting to go on to the next step, the beginning of the Quest on earth. The following poems illustrate the decision to leave the Oneness-existence, the unity of reality, and take incarnation. All these examples demonstrate the often-mantric quality of the style of Sri Chinmoy.

I Came

Into the world of beauty's flame,
Into the world of offering's game,
Into the world of lustre-flood,
I came, I came, my existence came.[7]

[6] Sri Chinmoy, *Lord, Receive This Little Undying Cry*, p. 28.

[7] Sri Chinmoy, *My Flute*, p. 36.

This example illustrates the highly-figurative language and unique stance of the speaker looking back on his own birth. These lofty metaphoric descriptions of the world surprise us and serve to retain nuances evocative of a different, higher level of conscious awareness. The compound nouns impart the perspective of ephemerality belonging to the manifestation of the Supreme in the physical world, but also transform our view of the solid world that we know into something wondrous. "Beauty's flame", a vital and dynamic image of beauty, also evokes the essence of purity; "offering's game" indicates the game of life entered into for the dedicated and self-offering it is to God the Creator – a sacrifice itself. And again, "lustre-flood", a much more intense and heightened vision of teeming life on earth, containing the reference to "Light", a further dimension of the divine spirit which moves therein, and creating an impression of a shimmering oneness of consciousness underlying physical reality.

Musically, the tone of this poem has a descending quality, emphasized by the slowing repetition of the final line, which mimics a descent from above. This last line also demonstrates a quiet power, an inevitability in the tone. It alludes to the progress of humanity through the evolution of the soul – "my existence came" – as though the persona is larger, the sum of past experiences, as well as future potentialities.

The seeming stylistic simplicity of Sri Chinmoy's lyrics, coupled with the expansiveness of themes is demonstrated further in the next two examples of the beginning of the Quest. Spatial and temporal dimensions are suspended in a moment's contemplation on the threshold of the quest for self.

The Forest of My Heart

I shall now call myself;
I shall now call.
In the forest of my heart, seeing myself,
I shall love myself and love myself.
I shall be my own quest,
My absolute wealth.
The journey of light supreme will commence
In the heart of freedom.[8]

In contrast to the commanding tone of *I Came*, this poem has that self-amorous tone reminiscent of much mystical and devotional poetry, both the tone and purpose illustrating an intensely private note of longing. The mood is softened again by a repetition, which brings a lilting rhythm. The first line repeated, which drops the last word, acquires a note of poignant tenderness or hesitancy. The repetition of the words "call" and "myself", coupled with the natural caesuras and pauses at line endings produce an ebb and flow reminiscent of the action of calling itself. The image of the heart as the path for the journey both reinforces the tenderness as well as emphasizing the inner journey, the surrender of all outer concerns, outer wealth. This represents a recognition now of the nature of the Quest, the journey, and the method of travel, is of an inner exploration, through love.

Again, the unknown of this inner quest is represented tentatively by the use of "forest of my heart", alluding to the singular, perhaps even untamed and dangerous nature of such

[8] J.M. and H. Roberts (eds.), *Selected Poetry of Sri Chinmoy*, p. 9.

an inner journey, and contrasts with the last line, the "heart of freedom". There is harmony and an almost musical unity, although there are also slight tensions between the resolution in the statement "I shall be my own quest" and the sweeter tenderness for the undertaking of this self for enlightenment. The voice of the author in the final statement reverts to the universal, enticing us to consider our own possibilities, to find our own heart of freedom.

It becomes increasingly evident that a major force within the poetry of Sri Chinmoy is metaphor, but a particular kind of metaphor. The following two poems demonstrate the different metaphoric levels in Sri Chinmoy's style. Both illustrate a consciousness fully aware of the lack of innocence in the world, which invokes the inner teaching of the Supreme through "silence". (Sri Chinmoy translated his own original Bengali poetry into English.)

Nikhil parane sakal paran
Ek abhinna jani
Tabu kena hai aparer prane
Aharaha ami hani
Amara sabai niyati bhritya
Lalate moder se kare nritya
Prashanti majhe niyati samadhi
Jani se gopan katha
Dhalo mor prane ogo ankhimani
Madhumoy nirabata.[9]

---

[9] Sri Chinmoy's original Bengali poems are sourced from www.srichinmoysongs.com

In the Universal Heart

In the universal heart all hearts are one,
    inseparable, I know.
Yet knowing this I hurt the hearts of others
    day and night.
We are all the slaves of fate;
It dances on our foreheads.
In peace sublime is the extinction-sleep of fate.
I know this secret.
O Jewel of my eye, pour into my heart
    Your golden Silence.[10]

Here the poet is demonstrating that knowledge alone is not enough for humanity; knowledge of the inseparable oneness portrayed by the image of humanity's heart moving as a unified force. The plaintive cry against the inevitability of human error underlies all human fate. This inevitability is arrested with the line "In peace sublime is the extinction-sleep of fate". If we consider the syntactical arrangement and the alliteration, which break the pace here, we find a seduction in their slowed and prolonged sounds – a way out of the traps of life, "the slaves of fate".

The sonority intimates that this peace is something solid, itself producing the demise of fate and "extinction-sleep" is not a violent, self-destruction image but a definite eclipse or escape, a transformation of this inevitable force. The contemplative mood is often broken in the last two lines as it is here by an invocation of a rhetorical nature. Moreover, there

[10] J.M. and H. Roberts op. cit., p. 2.

is an intricate metaphorical complexity in "Jewel of My Eye", as the intimate appellation referring to the Supreme as the Inner Guide, or the soul, which is to be found as the shining force resident in the "third eye" of the divine seeker. The use of the word "pour" lends a tangible reality to this succour, a molten quality to "Silence" reinforced by the adjective "golden", and altogether suggesting something both precious and solid over the emptiness usually associated with the word. It works very effectively as a mystical metaphor. The speaker is affirming, as he will over and again, that all of human care is obliterated only in the deep silence of meditation.

The theme of silence is again taken up in the following:

Child of Light

Yonder I hear in the depth of my heart
Your nectar-silence.
There shall be no problems,
No complications in my life anymore.
From now on I shall be the child of light
In the ocean of life,
And there my little boat is sailing,
Sailing with enormous delight.
My life is the game of hundreds of waves
In the great ocean of life.[11]

The compound noun "nectar-silence" is a key concept here, denoting the profound presence of the divine, but also something a little out of reach of human sensibility – perhaps

[11] J.M. and H. Roberts op. cit., p. 10.

a little unexpected – that the Supreme is both an intimate presence, and a little out of reach – yonder. In contrast to the previous poem, there is a moderating force in the tempo, rhythm and mood. The speaker is turning away from the world with its tentacles. The exhortation has been answered, the first step taken, though the wistfulness in that first recognition yonder demonstrates a vibration rather than a peal, underlined by the broken rhythm and half rhyme. Again the idea of "nectar-silence" suggests a nourishing, a sweetness and substance; it invites comparison with the idea of nectar as the food of the gods, with which perhaps the Supreme is tempting the speaker.

The tone develops with more confidence as the speaker takes up the theme of enlightenment – the inspired "child of light". And the metaphor of the ocean of life is extended; this single life as a boat sailing over the vastness of life, but with a newfound abandon and surrender. The use of the word "delight" transforms the old idea of a sea of troubles into something higher, a game of infinite varieties. There is a childlike evocation – an enjoyment of the play in the lyrical expression, it is a momentary illumination: life as a joyful challenge instead of a battle. In spite of the commonplace and the simplicity of expression, the poet's attitude here lifts the metaphorical level into the realm of the heart so that the reader identifies with the universal feeling of the poem.

So far the poems chosen have displayed an almost unconscious awareness of the quest within, whereas the fourth step in the Separation sequence – the awareness of the loss of oneness – exposes a more mature seeking, and this sophistication is characterized by the mind's limitations in view;

a perspective here as reminiscent of "the Fall". In the following three examples, the loss of Oneness with God can be seen to develop into the idea of the loss of the real Self.

Ki jena phelechhi kothai na jani haraye
Ta je thake chira ankhir arale palaye
Behu jug hate lukochuri khela khele
Shesh smriti tuku ajio pareni dhele

Hide and Seek

It seems that I have lost something somewhere.
My eyes are pining for it,
My heart is pining for it,
But it is all hidden.
From time immemorial
You have been playing hide and seek with me.
This much I can recollect, that's all.[12]

Here, the key theme of loss is instantly universalized, the loss is so significant and so deep that even the eyes are pining, and something deep within the reader's self responds with recognition and heartfelt sympathy. This blindness suggests the helplessness of the newborn, or human ignorance that is not even sure for what it seeks. The very soul is in darkness here, as the eyes are often invoked as the windows of the soul. There is a childlike vulnerability set against the mischievous, even cruel image of the Creator – deliberately hiding all – the sense of his playing a game with human beings over the millennia of creation. The final lines impart a feeling almost

[12] J.M. and H. Roberts op. cit., p. 36.

of despondency at the confusion of recollecting so little, at such reckless detachment on behalf of the benevolent One.

The rhetorical invocation in this next poem diminishes the vastness of distances in time to contrast with the present of the speaker, and is juxtaposed with the distance in spatial dimensions caused by the separation.

Shudhu seidin tomai dekhechhi
Khelechhi tomar sane
Janma labhechhi ama dhara bukhe
Tabu achhe mor mane
Charidike shudhu
Birajichhe smriti
Tumi aj bahu dure
Kanpichhe amar
Hridayer pakhi
Barai bedan sure

Only the Other Day

O Lord Supreme, only the other day
I saw You and played with You,
Before I came into the world of ignorance-night.
Yet I remember my golden past within and
without,
Alas, far, very far, now You are.
The bird of my heart is crying and trembling
with darkest pangs.[13]

[13] Sri Chinmoy, *My Flute*, p. 59.

A mystical framework is provided here by the nature of a unified golden past – an existence that alludes to a childlike nature of the Supreme playing perhaps in Elysian fields with the speaker. The poet often uses the motif of the world as the experience of "ignorance-night" for the soul, a dark experience in comparison with this gold of the other world, which again places the poem in the epic context for the human journey. The plaintive quality evident in the last few lines – very far, now You are – and the brokenly punctuated and reversed syntax gives a faltering, uncertain tone. The final metaphorical trope, "bird of my heart", the expression the poet uses to denote the inner aspiration, the soul, here also infers the fragility of the inner life as well as its intense suffering being separated in this physical world. Yet it also contains the suggestion of its albeit thwarted capacity to soar above all. The stark image of the vulnerability of the soul as a bird, is made all the more poignant with the ringing tone and rhyme in the line "crying and trembling", emphasizing not only inner pain, but "darkest pangs" of loss and suffering, a physical impression.

Labyrinth

A torturous road full of thorns;
At every step I encounter dire obstacles.
No light, no air, only a black shadow
  before me.
With a giant body he frightens me.
Alone I walk along an unlit, lightless
  labyrinth.
Long have I forgotten where my source is.[14]

---

[14] J.M. and H. Roberts, op. cit., p. 25.

The symbolic image of this lament indicates the psychological dramatization of the inner voyage and the blindness of the inner spiritual quest. This inner way is strewn with difficulties described metaphorically as material obstacles. "No light, no air" creates an aura of suffocation and the personification of a black shadow with a giant body evokes a real primal fear. The image of the shadow reinforces the idea of the psychological nature of the obstacles and that resistance to the light is in the physical mind. The alliteration and hard consonantal half rhymes in the last two lines first ring with the echo of footsteps as if on stone, then fade away with the image of a wanderer, completely separated and alienated. The innocence of the speaker is highlighted by the alarm of the imagery and the intensity of the mood created by the use of the sinister in the words "alone", "shadow", "giant" and "labyrinth". The distinction of the terms "unlit, lightless" is quite significant here, referring to both the outer pathway being unlit and the inner – the lack of inspirational or spiritual enlightenment.

The poet has shown this descent into ignorance, the danger of the human being forgetting where the source of light, of air, of comfort lies in human endeavour. This journey of the soul from human birth into the unlit physical plane of existence after separation from the divine light can be endless and touches on the theme of reincarnation, the vehicle of the soul's evolution. The following group of poems further illustrates this descent into loneliness and ignorance on the physical plane of existence. The use of short lyrics encapsulates a momentary idea or contemplation with an economy of language and imagery allowing the state of separation in the consciousness of the speaker to predominate.

Alo lagi ratri jagi
Shir tuliche sabuj lata
Kaligulir akulata
Jagalona prane amar
Kono byakulata
Ami shudhu ghumiye roy
Niye badhirata

To See the Light

To see the light
A tiny blade of grass
Remains wide awake all night.
To see the light
The buds offer their devoted eagerness.
Alas, neither a blade of grass nor the buds
Can awaken my aspiration-flame.
I sleep and sleep,
My ears tightly closed.[15]

Here a conceit is used to highlight the speaker's complete lack of inspiration to move toward the light. The lowly blade of grass and the buds are personified and endowed with a natural aspiration and yearning, in contrast to the speaker's own predicament. In the opening image, the key word "light" is operating on two levels, infusing the simple, life-sustaining necessity of the grass with patient humility and the eagerness of a seeker of enlightenment; and the buds with the spiritual quality of devotion. The second half of the lyric presents a

[15] J.M. and H. Roberts, op. cit., p. 11.

complementary and contrasting image – the speaker locked into himself and, with finality, eyes and ears "tightly closed", as if he were the bud, existing almost stubbornly only in his potentiality, forever without the energizing and illumining light. The poetic quality is in the aesthetic form: the two images fitting closely together illustrate the complete opposite of what should be – the absent human aspiration vs. even the instinctive nature of plants to respond to the spiritual allure of light. The compound noun "aspiration-flame" challenges the notion of passive receptivity of enlightenment, instead highlighting it to be a conscious and dynamic experience of fire reaching upward. But the prevailing image is that of the seeker's worth – as less even than a single blade of grass to awaken to this upward movement.

This recalls Walt Whitman, of course, who uses this conceit, the innate humility of grass, in his *Leaves of Grass*,[16] and extends it into a symbol to explore both the multiplicity and the oneness or unity of the world around him.

> Divine am I inside and out, and I make holy
> whatever I touch . . .
> If I worship any particular thing it shall be some of
> the Spread of my body.[17]

D.H. Lawrence has noted the tendency of Whitman's poetry to explore identification, which I differentiate from the Oneness

[16] Justin Kaplan (ed.), *Walt Whitman: Complete Poetry and Selected Prose*, p. 19.

[17] Justin Kaplan (ed.), *Walt Whitman: Complete Poetry and Selected Prose*, p. 51.

that Sri Chinmoy comprehends; yet Whitman does take the open road of experience, "the soul in her subtle sympathies accomplishing herself by the way".[18] This view of the soul journeying towards accomplishment does coincide with the themes of Sri Chinmoy, however it does not go quite so far.

> I visit the enclaves of God and look at the spheric
> product
> I look at quintillions ripened, and look at
> quintillions Green.[19]

Somehow these lines describe only the observer, a visitor to the realm of God, conveying a detachment far removed from the intimacy that Sri Chinmoy anticipates in the relationship.

The theme of the following final poems to illustrate the Separation is that of the difficulty in reconciling the material world in all its suffering with the perfection inherent in the divine. The treatment of this theme by Sri Chinmoy makes an interesting comparison with that of Snyder's "confrontation" within his poetic exploration of experiences in India. (See Snyder's poem below.)

The Waters of Peace

In how many ways You have sung
The song of liberation in my heart.
In return You have received only
unbearable pain.
I see all around me the heavy load of poverty

---

[18] D.H. Lawrence, *Studies in Classic American Literature*, pp. 173ff.

[19] Kaplan, op. cit., p. 63.

And the slumber of inconscience.
How can I lose myself in the waters of peace?[20]

The dramatization here is infused by both an apostrophe and a rhetorical question addressed to the Supreme, and the plaintive quality of the first four lines underlies the pain of the divine, as well as the seeker, due to his inability to respond to the "song of liberation". The seeker is caught in the ignorance of the human point of view, immobilizing poverty; an attitude only acknowledged by the human, where the poverty becomes a heavy load for the conscience because it is bereft of the spiritual light or illumination. The "slumber of inconscience" evokes a world unwilling to wake or to respond to the Supreme's song of liberation. The rhetorical question in the final line leaves us with a slightly ambivalent attitude, the waters of peace being both a plea for this as a resting place, a self-reprimand, or perhaps an accusation flung at the Supreme, depending upon the force and tone used in voicing it.

In the Wild Confusion-market

Suddenly he slipped away
From home
To embrace the life of solitude
And see the Face of God.
He saw God.
Where?
In the wild confusion-market
Of village-ignorance.[21]

---

[20] J.M. and H. Roberts, op. cit., p. 12.

[21] Sri Chinmoy, *Lord, Receive This Little Undying Cry*, p. 103.

This poem illustrates the coexistence of both God and ignorance in the world, through a revelation. "Suddenly" supports the immediacy of the image and the significance of the simple situation is to contrast the two paths of spirituality. The easy flow of alliteration in the first half corresponds to the easy path – the "life of solitude" – turning away from teeming humanity to find God, while the more difficult conceptual imagery of the compound nouns illustrates that this very complexity is precisely where God is to be found. The revelation is that God has to be found in all life, in all contexts – the transcendental concept is affirmed.

Salvation

If you think of sin,
    Then you need salvation.
If you think of ignorance,
    Then you need liberation.
If you think of oneness,
    Then you need God-realisation, Self-realisation.[22]

Here again the tiered structure of parallel concepts presents the three different world-views of examining "human error" or "frailty" as problem and solution. First, the traditional Western religious view with its allusion to sin, shown now in its modern context becomes slightly distasteful, negative and old fashioned. By contrast, the Eastern mystical view of liberation from ignorance, while it represents a much more palatable interpretation, is still only a middle-step on the ladder.

[22] Sri Chinmoy, *Lord, Receive This Little Undying Cry*, p. 90.

Then there is a significant change of key, a shift of emphasis in the final view as the poet/Master presents his own solution, a path which reconciles or even transcends the former two, that of the Oneness of all existence, which surpasses human moral dichotomies. "Oneness" transcends the problematic approaches, the assertion and solution are one and the same. Again there is a challenge to the reader that cannot be ignored because of the rhetorical structure of the poem, which once more channels the response back into the heart's contemplation of an aesthetically pleasing intuition – to rise above the lower levels for the higher aim of oneness. The reader can hardly resist the exhortation, claiming as his very own the poet's philosophy of the one source and goal of all humanity, in a way that supersedes the past irreconcilables of religion.

In contrast with the ideas of Sri Chinmoy, Gary Snyder viewed his encounter with India as a "Dantean journey into the underworld" and, according to Steuding, interpreted Mother Kali as a demonic, negative force.[23] He suffers a "shock of recognition" in India's philosophy and mythology, as "vast, touching the deepest areas of the mind",[24] but succumbs to the despair of the poverty and the crush of humanity. His poem entitled:

Mother of the Buddhas, Queen of Heaven,
Mother of the Sun; Marici, Goddess of the Dawn,

Opens with:

old sow in the mud
bristles caked black
down her powerful neck

[23] Bob Steuding, *Gary Snyder*, p. 123.

[24] Gary Snyder, *Earth House Hold*, p. 114.

tiny hooves churn
squat body slithering
deep in food dirt.

And ends with:

she turns her small eye
from earth to
look up at me.[25]

Sri Chinmoy explains his point of view thus:

> If we go deeper into ignorance we see it is all a play of inconscience. . . . To enter into ignorance is to take a negative path. The best way, the positive way is to follow the path of light. Enter into illumination first.[26]

Snyder falls into the common Western view of Kali as a dark force, whereas Sri Chinmoy's view allows the necessity for destruction prior to transformation, into the possibilities of a new incarnation.

In this chapter, we have seen how the simple style of the lyrics of Sri Chinmoy masks a quite complex and consummate poetic skill. The free verse and the cryptic tendencies of the language, often utilizing the techniques of rhetoric and coupled with the mantric mode of speech, give the diction a most unusual quality of authority. Together with the use of both linguistic and ideational parallels and equivalences, sometimes tier upon tier, the poetry has a symmetrical precision, which adds authoritative weight to the revelatory nature of the subject

---

[25] Gary Snyder, *The Black Country*, p. 92.

[26] Sri Chinmoy, *Samadhi and Siddhi*, Introduction.

matter. In other cases, the verse can be looser, relying on a more contemplative mood or tone for poetic effect. Although I have imposed the complex schemata of The Ever-Transcending Quest on the poet's work, I hope it will become clearer as we explore the next chapter – The Trial – that this is a valid inroad to the understanding of such a vast body of work that expands our understanding of both spiritual themes and the human spiritual journey.

2

The Trial

IN CHAPTER 1 we followed the development of The Ever-Transcending Quest through the theme of Separation from the Divine and deepened our understanding of the philosophy of the evolution of the soul that is expounded throughout the writings of Sri Chinmoy. The Trial now explores the steps of the mature spiritual aspirant as he is tested and the intricacies of the profound inner relationship and interaction with the Supreme Consciousness.

Trial

- Trials begin
- Despair and loss of faith
- Intervention of God's Compassion
- Nearing the Goal
- Final Temptation

The motifs I have chosen to study in this chapter are by no means an exhaustive guide for a seeker in The Ever-Transcending Quest. The subtle relationship between a seeker and his God can involve many cycles of union and subsequent falls, extremely high experiences, with the interplay of human doubts and insecurities. There is also the role of humility, of sincerity, of faith and, indeed, of gratitude which Sri Chinmoy has on many occasions stated holds all of the divine qualities. The vastness of the work, as well as the theme, dictates that some restrictions must be imposed. Nevertheless, we can use the steps of the Trial to gain an insight into the intensity of love and longing for this final consummation of Oneness in Consciousness that the seeker is inwardly compelled to pursue.

Many of these lyrics demonstrate a complex and interesting use of repetition, as well as an artful interrelationship between poems that follow the same theme. There is often a shift in tone or point of view between poems, or even within a single poem. Some of the lyrics that describe these steps in the development of the seeker's inner journey illustrate the darker side of human nature drawn from quite a different perspective. The portrayal of the "enemies within" by Sri Chinmoy is one of profound spiritual insight. He dramatizes the confusing battleground of the forces of man's animal past set against his higher aspirations, and in so doing shines a light on our particular position in a continuum of human evolution. Far from accepting that we are now the culmination of millions of years of evolution, Sri Chinmoy indicates that we have yet much distance to cover, and that the ultimate goal of humanity far surpasses our wildest expectations.

The teachings of Sri Chinmoy rest on the idea of consciousness at the core of the self: that there is a centre of presence belonging to each major part of the being, which will try to influence or dominate the whole. On a very basic level, the individual can be swayed or directed by these separate parts or levels of the consciousness. Without delving too deeply into the philosophical panoply of Hinduism, which outlines the system of *chakras* (centres of energy) in the body, it does help that Sri Chinmoy has explained these aspects of the self extensively in his writings. Sri Chinmoy maintains that a human being is composed of five major parts. The soul, which is perfected and stands at the pinnacle or head of a family collective. Then follow the heart, the mind, the vital and the physical body itself. These parts of the being are subordinate to the soul and can be characterized in both positive and negative terms according to their level of development.

Each centre, according to Sri Chinmoy, has an important role to play in life's evolution, as well as having a more, or less illumined nature, culminating in the soul at the zenith. It is the soul which is meant to direct or lead the other parts of the being as the soul's consciousness is directly linked to the One, the highest Supreme or the Universal Consciousness. However, in practice we do not always allow the soul to lead. For example, the body consciousness can be well disciplined, or it can be steeped in lethargy. The mind can be positive and optimistic, inclined toward the intellect or alternately pessimistic and negative, obsessed with the mundane. On the other hand, the vital consciousness, the seat of the emotions, can be the source of both desire, or of aggression as well as being the fount of dynamism, the driving force in life. Whereas the heart centre, being oriented closest to the soul, and most influenced by the divinity of the soul, is portrayed as the safest and the most advantageous place for the seeker to begin his spiritual journey through meditation and, indeed, to be directed forward in life from this safe harbour. This is due to the heart's qualities and ability to completely identify itself with the higher consciousness of the soul and to become one with the soul's higher will and purpose.

We can go some way in understanding this model by looking at the following series of poems taken, I must say, from a vast array of Sri Chinmoy's poetry on these themes. These exhortations, addressed to God, seem on the surface to be a light-hearted and quite humorous treatment of that interaction which is really of intensely serious significance to the seeker facing inner trials. They both portray and illustrate the conflicting elements in an individual's psyche in a quite revelatory way.

My Body Tells You

My body tells You, Lord,
Not to scold me.
My body feels that I need
A little more rest.
I tell You, Lord,
That if I am allowed
To get up at my own time
    I shall love You,
    I shall serve You,
    I shall even glorify You.[1]

The inner battle is delineated here with the urging of the body consciousness in its most unwilling and immovable aspect, lethargy; and it reveals its own inherent weakness, never to be

[1] Sri Chinmoy, *Lord, Receive This Little Undying Cry*, p. 8.

satisfied. Here we have the strains of a faltering anapest, cut short abruptly with the emphatic sentence endings in the second and fourth lines. Tension is created between the exhortations upward to alleviate God's strictness, and the indulgence of the body for ever-more rest which brings us down again. The demands of the body appear plausible, yet the speaker reveals himself to be in thrall to this indulgent persona. The reasoned plea for just a little more rest, while innocent, childlike, even humorous, rings hollow in light of the exaggerated promises at the close. There is the plea to the Lord, but also a surreptitious nod at a wider Self, that self who may wake up several hours later and bemoan the loss of time perhaps? The use of the adverb "even" while pointing to the inflated promise, gives emphasis to the speaker's own self-deception; helplessly caught between the body, and the necessity of rising for the ritual of worship. The repetitions at the close are ambiguously reverent and ironical, enticing the reader into self-recognition of human weakness, and an inevitable complicity for the need of a divine scolding in a neat circular motion.

Scolding Is not a Healthy Experience

My mind tells You, Lord,
To scold me in private
If You really have to.
I need not tell You, Lord,
That scolding is not a healthy experience
For the one who scolds
Nor for the one who is being scolded.[2]

[2] Sri Chinmoy, *Lord, Receive This Little Undying Cry,* p. 9.

Again, here as the mind is separated from the true self it is revealed as the culprit, but there is also the recognition of our complete and unconscious identification with the mind. As the surreptitious tone unfolds, we recognize that the mind can be crafty. The point of view becomes self-illumining, as this propensity for trickery or treachery in the mind's self-justification is plotted alongside its plea for discretion. We have to suspect the persona, which aims to avoid any kind of exposure or humiliation at all costs. Indeed, the insinuating tone, appealing through its misguided reasoning, emerges ironically as an audacious reproach to God Himself. The mind is betrayed in the self-serving final line, placing itself and God on equal terms in this amusing exchange. We are left with an image that slips between the pompous, and perhaps a little handwringing at its own effrontery.

Scolding Does No Good

My vital tells You, Lord,
Not to scold me.
I know I always do something wrong,
But when You scold me
It does me no good.
After all, who has changed his life
By being scolded?
No one!
Therefore, love me, Lord,
Love me even more,
Especially when You are tempted to scold me.[3]

---

[3] Sri Chinmoy, *Lord, Receive This Little Undying Cry,* p. 10.

The appeal from the vital here reveals the histrionics of a wild and unbridled child. Under the mantle of the simple, childlike language is the most marvellous play of this wilful and unrepentant part of the being, "After all, who has changed his life/By being scolded?" The demanding and recalcitrant nature of the vital predominates and its reasoning illustrates the futility of any kind of chastisement in order to assuage and deflect responsibility. As it appeals to God for His infinite Compassion, the vital reveals its own intransigence, and we must witness and recognize the limitations of our own occasional stubbornness.

This series of poems slowly builds for us a defined, characteristic pattern of each part of the inner being and how they can influence and even manipulate us. The poet, by taking the reader through these first three stages, has forced an impasse by undermining the authority of the body, the mind and the vital. To whom, then, does the reader appeal for guidance or what part of the inner self can be trusted? Sri Chinmoy then makes a comparison with the level of the heart-consciousness. As we are led into the heart's offering we observe in its plea a complete change of tone, and being the last poem in the group, it adds considerable weight to the message. To the reader, the heart's appeal seems a clear contrast in its openness and honesty, and its impact is quite profound.

My Heart Tells You to Scold Me

My heart tells You, Lord,
To scold me when I do anything wrong.
What both of us want from my life
Is perfection-delight;

Therefore, Lord, scold me.
I deserve it; I need it.
My sense of perfection
Badly needs it.[4]

The striking contrast in tone produces an immediate impact on the reader of the sincerity, humility and higher authority of the heart. By engaging the reader in the former self-recognition of a hierarchy that is deficient in its devotion, the poet elicits our acknowledgement of the heart's capacity as the superior authority on the inner path to enlightenment. It is the heart, closest to the purity and the integrity of the soul, which is demonstrated as the only reliable and safe guide. In addition, the poem closes on the only note that *is* likely to kindle the Compassion of the Supreme. This adds to the weight of the superiority of the heart and its supremacy over the other parts of the inner self.

The strophic structure turns the theme back on the opening idea of the necessity for the situation – the divine scolding; and the satire on rhetoric is thus put to good use in these pieces, evoking human sympathy at the same time as it is indicating a higher, more illumined point of view. Furthermore, the use of the term "scold" takes on increasingly more significance through the series, developing from undertones of a harsh parent, until by the end it is the compassionate indulgence of a lenient guide, deftly supplanting outdated religious ideas of God as judge or punisher of human error with the idea of God as helper or facilitator on the path to self-knowledge and perfection.

[4] Sri Chinmoy, *Lord, Receive This Little Undying Cry,* p. 11.

A great deal of Sri Chinmoy's poetry can be read as an extended exhortation to the reader to "know yourself". Sri Chinmoy emphasizes the extent of our ignorance about the inner worlds within us in this excerpt from his lecture "Know Thyself":

> *Atmanam viddhi* – Know thyself. Each individual has to know himself. He has to know himself as the infinite, eternal and immortal Consciousness. The concept of Infinity, Eternity and Immortality is absolutely foreign to us. Why? The reason is quite simple. We live in the body, rather than in the soul. To us the body is everything. There is nothing and can be nothing beyond the body. The existence of the soul we consider sheer imagination. But I assure you that the soul is not imaginary. It is at once the life and the revelation of the Cosmic Reality.[5]

Sri Chinmoy further explores the theme of the mind as an obstacle to be distrusted on the inner journey in the following short poem, which is full of challenge to a Western sensibility that has been taught the "man of science" is the pinnacle of civilization:

Never Believe What Your Mind Says

Never believe what your mind says.
Your mind is a liar.

Never believe what your mind says.
Your mind is a beggar.

Never believe what your mind says,

---

[5] Sri Chinmoy, Lecture "Know Thyself", University of Puerto Rico, printed in *The Inner Promise,* Simon & Schuster, 1974, p. 22.

Your mind is secretly digging your grave.

Never believe what your mind says.
Your mind tells you that God is somewhere else,
That God is someone else other than you.[6]

Sri Chinmoy uses his favoured technique – a group of related emphatic statements, aphorisms that explore and delineate the mind's limitations, each level building on the last to a final illuminating point. At first, the reader might react with surprise and even alarm: "a liar", "a beggar"? These are strong and confronting statements, for almost all of us identify quite closely, indeed indiscriminately, with the mind as the self. Nevertheless, the insistent and compelling repetition is seductive and, by the third stanza, "secretly digging your grave", we begin to be drawn into doubt. We are invited to recognize, albeit reluctantly, this negative propensity of the mind, the uncertainty and vacillation, the fears and anxieties that wear us out, worry us "to death", the "nails in the coffin" as it were. We recall our own experiences with the often-perplexing dilemma of being in "two minds" and we are perhaps ready to hear the speaker out.

The close of the poem then achieves an easy triumph. Having been compelled into a gentle admission of the mind's continual dialectic as self-limiting or self-defeating, we are now presented with our own real Self, the divinity within. We have learned as children that "the Kingdom of Heaven is within"; we are called back to this truth in spite of the mind's critical

---

[6] Sri Chinmoy, *When God Love Descends,* p. 28.

tendency to reason it away. This final appeal is both aesthetically pleasing and of inarguable clarity – that we are in fact God, and it challenges the reader to a reappraisal of the "self", by bringing him out of the mind, and into the higher vision of the poet. The mind can now be seen for what it is, one of the trials to be overcome: the trial of self-doubt. The reader is led back to the instinctive feeling of a truth that can only be perceived inwardly. It is both affirmation and revelation combined.

Sri Chinmoy's extraordinary rhetorical power is illustrated further in the following poem. The reader is again enticed into a new awareness of the divine by a confrontation with the human weakness of fear. The mind's fear becomes another significant trial in the seeker's inner journey towards the truth of his real nature.

I Am Afraid of Beauty

I am afraid of earth-beauty.
    It is nothing but ugliness.

I am afraid of Heaven-beauty.
    It seems it is all-devouring power.

I am afraid of God Beauty.
    It tells me that it will eclipse
    My long-treasured individuality.[7]

Oddly enough, the solemnity of tone is undercut by the emerging timidity of fear itself, which is inherent in the repetition. As we progress from the certainty and rejection in

[7] Sri Chinmoy, *Lord, Receive This Little Undying Cry,* p. 6.

the opening, "it is nothing but ugliness", to the interpretation of "it seems", to the final note of distrust of the persona "it tells me" at the close, we begin to see an abstraction, an absurdity. The attitude of the speaker illustrates a point of view that is simultaneously aware of a higher point of view, but keeps withdrawing from it through fear. The compound noun "earth-beauty" framed between fear and ugliness is constrained. It brings us up short when we expect to soar at the splendours of the creation itself. This juxtaposition through the eyes of fear illustrates the faltering human steps and misapprehensions of the spiritual vision by focusing on the timid and negative.

Nevertheless, the oft-quoted view of the world reality as ugly is too simplistic, ungenerous and pessimistic here. We have to mistrust this persona. Again, the vision presented as "Heaven-beauty" proposes another level of existence, a glimpse of the beauty of another, an ethereal world of the immortal soul, but the image is rendered incongruous by the attributed "all-devouring power". We are once again questioning this stance with our own confidence that Heaven *must* be a benevolent power. The antithesis of "God-beauty" is also envisioned through the persona of fear. This fear of the loss of individuality expresses one of the innermost insecurities common to humanity, fear of annihilation. However, there is a simultaneous call to another inner instinct of humanity for unity, for enlargement. The tension between the two viewpoints snaps and we respond by recoiling from the limitations. We recognize our own weaknesses, we also recognize the challenge to fear as an undignified and unworthy motivation. It is an open invitation, indeed a challenge to put aside fear and aspire to the ideal of oneness on a heroic scale.

The reader here is once more compelled to summon his or her own inner depths of faith in the search for a real and deeper truth. This key technique of leading the reader constantly to appraise and reassess his own inner spiritual assumptions and responses recurs over and again in much of the poetry. It is only apparent by extensive reading of the work just how persuasive and influential on the psyche of the reader this can be.

The Trial now enters another level: as ignorance and alienation overcome the seeker, he enters into the dangerous territory of despair and loss of faith. It is again of interest to recall Snyder's verse here, particularly those poems he wrote after visiting India, though it would seem that Snyder's observations have their genesis more in a political context. He says:

> It became clear that "Hinduism" and "Buddhism" as social institutions had long been accomplices of the State in burdening and binding people, rather than serving to liberate them.[8]

The following lyric by Sri Chinmoy, however, addresses the unknowability of the Divine in purpose and intention, emphasizing the limits of the human point of view in the midst of darkness:

Beyond My Imagination

In the temple, in the mosque, there is no light.
How can I believe that this is what God wants?
How can God allow His children to be helpless,

[8] Gary Snyder, *Earth House Hold*, pp. 114-15.

Orphaned, lame and destitute?
I know not.
It is beyond my imagination.[9]

Here we can also find anguish and despair, but no underlying bitterness, as in the assumptions of Snyder. Instead there is as well as perturbation, a humble acceptance, even wonder. Initially, there is disbelief, and we can feel a painful railing against the seeming injustice of God's detachment. Then, in his lament, the poet must surrender to the unknowable. The two simple statements at the end, with their brevity and finality, ending with the word "imagination", somehow give the piece an open ending, swinging between despair and vaster, uncharted realms. Is the poem pointing a finger at this despair or is it simply indicating the unfathomable divine purpose?

Read in this order, the poems lead us with deepest feeling into the seeker's decline, and this next poem reflects on the knowledge of loss in the inner world. It seems to be expressing the seeker's overwhelming anguish and puzzlement at being found bereft of his usual companion of faith.

I Know not Why

My mind suffers badly
Because I do not invoke You.
Alas, I cry and weep.
Insufferable are my pangs,
Yet I know not why I do not long for You.[10]

---

[9] Sri Chinmoy, *Lord, Receive This Little Undying Cry*, p. 261.

[10] Ibid., p. 160.

The seeming simplicity of this lyric disguises a more formalized anguish. Again we are removed from the mind, the mind is the sufferer, and yet the language offers an unparalleled depth of heartfeeling. The archaic cry "alas", the long syllabic "insufferable", and the vibration of "pangs", which are then organized around the seeker's reticence, echo the helplessness and hopelessness of his inability to fathom why there is still no longing. We can read between the lines and see that for the seeker, it is the longing in itself that will bring relief; therefore, his intransigence is all the more pitiable. This formality is emphasized in the syntax of the final line and recalls other poets who have used this distancing device. Emily Dickinson writes:

> After great pain, a formal feeling comes–
> The Nerves sit ceremonious, like Tombs–
> The stiff Heart questions was it He, that bore,
> And Yesterday, or Centuries before? . . .[11]

We can see here that same cavern of emptiness and inertia. The following lyric by Sri Chinmoy also illustrates a haunting message of the seeker's despair presented with a series of rhetorical questions. Their imploring tone tails off wistfully at the close without resolution.

> *Kar parashe kumud hase*
> *Nayan khule kali*
> *Kahar shobha jhare pare*
> *Jyochna haye gali*
> *Ke se amar nayan mani*

---

[11] Thomas H. Johnson (ed), *Final Harvest: Emily Dickinson's Poems,* p. 73.

Praner priyatama
Swapne kena dekhina se
Anan manorama

By Whose Touch

By whose touch does the lily smile
And open its beauty-bud?
Whose moonlit beauty
Do I see in the lily?
Who is the Eye of my eye;
Who is the Heart of my heart?
Alas, then why do I not see Him,
His Face of transcendental Beauty,
Even in my dreams?[12]

In the opening image the relationship between the lily and the moon is portrayed with poignant and ethereal beauty – the moon being an expression of the divine animating quality of light and the lily responding by blossoming with a satisfying smile. This intimacy portrayed between a simple flower and the divine is then contrasted with the seeker's corresponding lack; an inconsolable alienation from this source of love. The longing for intimacy – the divine touch – imparts an envious hunger to the speaker. The simple presence and instinct of the life-force in the lily contrasts with the complicated fluctuating presence and absence in the human seeker; but the surpassing beauty of the divine is withheld. It not only admits of the perception of the divine in the human, but also of the divine as the perceptor; God and human as One,

[12] J.M. & H. Roberts, op. cit., p. 6.

"Who is the Eye of my eye; / Who is the Heart of my heart?" The plaintive cry at the close places the lily back into unconscious nature by accentuating humanity's conscious aspiration and search for divinity. However, at the same time we understand the futility of expecting to apprehend the divine through the reason of the mind or even of the senses. We are left with the impression of helplessness, grasping at straws, at the mercy of capricious dreams.

The ultimate expression of the fall into despair is attained in the following poem. Although it speaks indifferently of the loss of faith and direction, the point of view is undercut by a subtle self-irony at the close.

Nai je kichhui nai
Dekhabar mato shunabar mato
Nai je kichhui nai
Sadhan bhajan dhyan aradhan
Nai je kichhui nai
Charidike achhe shudhu hahakar
Dhuli kardama chhai
Bishai basana swalpe tushti
Nai je kichhui nai.

I Have Nothing

I have nothing.
I have nothing to show or tell.
I have no spirituality, no worship,
No meditation, no adoration;
Nothing.
Around me are only inner pangs and
frustrations,

Dust, clay and ash.
I am satisfied with the world of
    matter and desire.
I am compelled to be satisfied with little,
    very little.
I have nothing.[13]

Paradoxically, the enveloping structure and short, sharp repetitions seem to express both dread and defiance in the face of the seeker's failure in the spiritual quest. The emotionless phrasing draws us into the undertone of stress to the point of paralysis. And yet the seeker, when turning back to the secular world of matter and desire, and forced to compare it with the wealth of the spiritual life of worship, adoration and meditation, must find it wanting. It is the world of matter and desire, which are characterized as the "little, very little" at the close. The low pitch and cutting sense of rhythm and assonantal half-rhyme express the overwhelming sense of loss as a cry from the abyss. The chanting tone gives emphasis to the oblivion caused by the loss of spiritual aspiration at this level: "I am *compelled* . . ." illustrates both a position of stubbornness as much as a position that has been forced onto the seeker; he is cornered. The spiritual life, strewn with pain and failure, has been put aside. There seems no way out. Yet there is still a sense that this seeker is not really satisfied with the dust, clay and ash of a faltering spirituality.

This poem illustrates the seeker at his lowest ebb. The "dust, clay and ash" gives us a powerful impression of the

[13] Sri Chinmoy, *The Garden of Love-Light,* p. 42.

bitter taste of failure. It is now that the Grace of the Supreme Being must intervene to once again motivate the seeker. This intervention of the Supreme's own Will allows the seeker to realise and experience divine Compassion before the quest can be continued. This is not, however, a passive stage by any means. As the lyrics illustrate, there has to be a complex interaction between the seeker and God the Supreme to overcome despair.

The descent of divine Compassion is characterized by the following two poems. As an expression of interior meditations on the nature of divine Compassion, they effectively bring forward the humility of the speaker like an action and its subsequent response. Sri Chinmoy again uses a simple metaphorical trope to expand the language into metaphysical expression. The inner experiences on the threshold of the highest human achievement of the divine, as here expressed by the poet, take the reader empathetically upward to a new level of awareness, both of the power of humility, and of the nature of the relationship with God.

Jadi bhabi toma dakibona ar
Heribona oi mukh
Nayan mudiya thakibo niyata
Tahate paiba sukh
Sahasa tomar hasir lahari
Shune dekhi ankhi khule
Ati kachhe priya asiyacha aj
Najani kemane bhule.

Waves of Your Smile

If and when I think that I shall not
invoke You any more,
I shall not even look at You,
But shall keep my eyes shut
And thus derive happiness,
I see You touching my eyes
With the waves of Your Smile.
I know not, Beloved, how and why
You are so close to me today.
Perhaps all this is just a mistake.[14]

Here we witness the seeker at his lowest ebb, shunning aspiration itself. The petulance of the child, eyes tightly shut, and stilted tone of the opening, blossoms into wonder as despair gives way under the confrontation with the image "waves of Your Smile". This metaphorical expression is commonly used by Sri Chinmoy to characterize a communication from the Supreme and suggests both a permeation, as of radio waves, as well as a palpable interaction. The image of the touch of the eyes with the waves of God's own Consciousness seems to have the effect of magically opening them to the Light. It captures for us the rapturous encounter with divine Grace.

The seeker is seen to respond simultaneously with humility, surrender and bewilderment. The slow movement of syntax, postponing the main clause, mimics the reawakening of the seeker's spirit. As it builds up to the powerful image of supreme Compassion, the artificial resistance of the opening is

---

[14] J.M. and H. Roberts, op. cit., p. 17.

transformed into the intimate acknowledgement of endearment and mystery at the close. Human nature, just as apt to ask "what have I done right?" as "what have I done wrong?", can never fathom this divine Grace.

It is interesting to note that both Whitman and Snyder also use the symbolism of the sea as an aspect of God's presence, its liquidity serving to characterize the permeation of consciousness or peace. Snyder's poem, "Burning Island" makes an interesting comparison here:

> O Wave God who broke through me today

Then, as it slips into a series of word associations, it seems to lose its intimacy,

> Gods tides capes currents
> flows & spirals of
> pool & powers[15]

While behind the vision of Snyder is the idea of Oneness, he is more often concerned with the social order and gets caught up in the outer world, rather than the inner. Molesworth makes a note that Snyder's vision is actually limited by his reformist function,[16] while, in comparison, Sri Chinmoy is more interested in communicating a vision of God which is both deeply intimate and expansive at the same time.

In the next poem, Sri Chinmoy illustrates that the battering a spiritual seeker receives from a sceptical and negative world can actually be softened and diffused by the descent of divine Compassion.

---

[15] Gary Snyder, *Regarding Wave,* p. 33.

[16] Charles Molesworth, *Gary Snyder's Vision,* p. 32.

Your Compassion-Power

When I am insulted,
When I am humiliated,
You strengthen me with Your Compassion-Power.
You come to me carrying the dawn in Your Hands
To replace my life of sorrow.
My heart's secret tears
Create endless sufferings in Your Heart.
I know one day You will come to me;
Therefore, today everything that I have and am
Is dancing with joy.[17]

This experience of compassion is portrayed as interactive rather than passive; the blessing producing the response of strengthening the seeker to be an effective agent in the world. Life is renewed and even replaced, "You come to me carrying the dawn in Your Hands". How can the reader ever fathom the mysteries that the Supreme is giving the seeker here? The beauties of the universe, the creative life-force itself is hinted at, as the Supreme comes with humility, with His All, to give to the seeker in exchange for his "life of sorrow". The human dimension is transported out of the insignificance of a modern philosophical context, as an individual in a meaningless universe, and carried into the realms of the divinely heroic. In this poem, God becomes the servant in His own Divine Lila, and the tears of humanity are not separate, but God's own. The form of the poem – short, sharp, self-referencing lines, alternating with longer lines indicating God – gives an unusual rhythmic

[17] J.M. and H. Roberts, op. cit., p. 43.

outreaching effect and confirms the extra dimension that has been given to the seeker by the presence of the divine in his life. The poem ends on a note of quivering optimism for the union to come.

The following lyric on compassion also touches on some of the keystones of Sri Chinmoy's more Eastern philosophic teachings: of reincarnation, the evolution of consciousness, and of God and man as equal partners.

I Butchered Your Ignorance

When I thought I was the doer
Of all my deeds,
I turned to mist,
I died.
I became the emperor of giant failures.
My soul came to the fore,
Consoled my visionless ignorance.
God made His Appearance supreme
"You fool, be not wedded to impossibility's
    lifeless beauty.
I waste not a leaf.
I butchered your ignorance wild for you
To equal My Transcendental Throne."[18]

These short, emphatic statements of confession by the human speaker at the opening seem feeble and are in stark contrast with the power and colour of the speech of God at the close. Here we see the strongest and most startling expression of man's delusion: first that he is alone and second that only he is responsible for his

[18] Sri Chinmoy, *The Dance of Life,* p. 35.

actions. Here we witness the refutation of existential man, containing the visionless ego, who becomes "the emperor of giant failures" when divorced from his divinity. Even the choice of the word "emperor" recalls that greatest of conquerors who seemed to overreach himself in the end. God finally comes forward to ordain man with his *raison d'être*. In fact, God states emphatically that it is absurd to think of the two as separate: "impossibility's lifeless beauty", as though man were indeed simply a body of lifeless clay without the divine animating force.

As with many of these poems, the particularity of the poet's own experience is blended with the universality of the lyric "I" with which the reader identifies. As the poem progresses into an intimate and powerful reprimand by God, the reader participates in the ensuing transformation, becoming aware of the height of his own Goal in all of humanity's destiny. This is a strong example of Sri Chinmoy's consummate lyrical process of organizing the experience from each different perspective into an experience of growth and illumination.

Elsewhere in his writings, Sri Chinmoy emphasizes that the soul is divine, the soul is the representative of God the Supreme, and that the Supreme can and does speak through this vessel. Over and again we witness Sri Chinmoy taking great pains to update these ancient Vedic truths for Western sensibilities, that human beings need to recognize the reality of their divinity and the One Consciousness that we share:

> Man and God are eternally one. Like God, man is infinite; like man, God is finite. There is no yawning gulf between man and God. Man is the God of tomorrow; God, the man of yesterday and today.[19]

---

[19] Sri Chinmoy, *Yoga and the Spiritual Life*, p. 1.

So we see in the former poem the different levels of the being delineated. First, the initial recognition that it is the Supreme who is living and acting through the physical manifestation of life on earth; that the Supreme is ultimately both the doer and receiver of all actions and consequences. This is a common theme in the ancient Hindu writings, indeed it is the fundamental lesson of Krishna's lecture to Arjuna on the battlefield of Kurukshetra in *Mahabharata*. Second, that the key to the pathway of transformation is the soul, the Inner Pilot as Sri Chinmoy terms it, and God's spokesperson as it were. Third, the reference here to Kipling, "I waste not a leaf",[20] in which Sri Chinmoy recalls the kernel of his own philosophic truth of the reincarnation of souls for the evolutionary process. Finally, inherent in the pronouncement of God is that familiar thread that it is God who is guiding the Cosmic Game, that He is the one who has raised humanity from the animal world, and will be the one to raise humanity into the next level of evolution, to equal His own Consciousness. It is an

[20] I quote Sri Chinmoy's own reference in a public lecture "Is Death the End", University of Kent, Canterbury on 11 November 1970, printed in *The Inner Promise,* p. 167:

"Kipling's immortal utterance runs:

They will come back, come back again,
  As long as the red Earth rolls.
  He never wasted a leaf or a tree
  Do you think he would squander souls?

Each incarnation is leading us toward a higher life, a better life. We are in the process of evolution. Each incarnation is a rung in the ladder. . . . Man is progressing consciously and unconsciously. . . ."

extraordinary achievement in such a short piece.

With the operation of divine Compassion, the seeker is now able to make faster progress in the Trial towards his goal of God-Realisation or Self-Realisation. The following group of three poems is chosen to illustrate the state of the seeker as he once more begins his journey, aspiring towards spiritual union with his Beloved. They demonstrate the poet's skill with a language that is not his native tongue, with simple direct statements, expressing this new faith and assurance on the inner journey.

Ghuche geche ama nisha
Peyechhi tomar disha
Amar hriday majhe
Ki jani ki jadu achhe
Gharidike marubhumi
Nahi tabu mor trisha

The Dark Night

The dark night has at last ended.
I have now seen You
Inside the depth of my heart.
I do not know what magic abides inside me.
Around me is the desert,
Yet I am not parched with thirst.[21]

The poem's strength is in its calm and considered acceptance, as if after a long storm. There is also a humble expression of wonderment at the realisation that the divine goal, the prize is actually near, indeed to be found within. It intimates this

[21] J.M. and H. Roberts, op. cit., p. 26.

revelation with quiet certitude. The poem acknowledges a partial enlightenment that there is indeed magic within. In addition there is the allure, the promise of the unknown depths yet to be discovered. The eternal and recurring motif that what man seeks is himself is restated with a new emphasis, a new simplicity, and all else is relegated to the desert. At last for the seeker, here is a truly thirst-quenching, fulfilling knowledge. Again I quote from Sri Chinmoy's philosophic writings where he indicates that this attainment of the highest is by no means a passive action, but instead relies upon an intricate relationship between human aspiration and divine revelation:

> Who is God? God is an infinite Consciousness. He is also the self-illumining Light. There is no human being who does not own within himself this infinite Consciousness and this self-illumining Light. God is not something to be obtained from outside. God is that very thing which can be unfolded from within.[22]

The next poem also beautifully illustrates the poet's simplicity in expressing these tentative forays into illumination and into a state of union with the highest consciousness:

The Swing of Delight

Hope-river flows, hope-river flows.
In the lap of the unknown
Is the river of smile.
At every moment I cry and weep with hope;
Again, it is I who dance with my Lord
In the swing of delight.[23]

[22] Sri Chinmoy, *Yoga and the Spiritual Life*, p. 7.

[23] J.M. and H. Roberts, op. cit., p. 27.

The imagery here is so strongly characterized – hope as a flowing river – it induces the heart of the reader to leap. After the drought of despair, the reader can both visualize and participate in the experience of the release of tension into the flood of the Infinite Consciousness. The divine Being characterized as a river of smile, the associations with the purity of water, the flowing nature of consciousness, blend into the notes of happiness and unbridled joy. The seeker is carried along on this river of hope, after the long and bitter struggle, into a realm where delight swings us into the air. The lap of the unknown, with its tones of a maternalistic or paternalistic aura embracing the child, gives us an image of a divine Parent playing and dancing with us. Bennett[24] often notes that Sri Chinmoy formulates a new mode of expression to characterize these unfamiliar states of the higher consciousness, a form so simple that it belies its scope.

In comparison, however, the following poem illustrates a more mature and emphatic assurance of the meeting place between the seeker and God that is to come.

Our Meeting Place

O Lord, my Master-Love, how far are we,
How far from ecstasy's silence-embrace?
Heavy is my heart with sleepless sighs and pangs;
I know my bleeding core, our meeting place.[25]

---

[24] V.M. Bennett, *Simplicity and Power: The Poetry of Sri Chinmoy, 1971-1981*, Aum Publications, 1991.

[25] Sri Chinmoy, *My Flute,* p. 46.

This lyrical invocation expresses a dramatic, meditative plea to the Supreme from the seeker nearing the end of his journey. The tone is impatient with anticipation, as the seeker has already claimed his "Master-Love". In the marriage of these two terms, Master is softened, and love is validated; Love becomes the Master and the metaphor for God-union and the promise of blissful fulfilment. A state, constant but not static, is evoked by the term "ecstasy's silence-embrace" and a deepening, uplifting movement is imparted to the image. The pace with its steadiness and stresses in the centre of lines produces an inexorable rhythm. There are further syllabic delays in the third line, which break the cadence and accentuate the feeling of heaviness, of plodding. The final emphasis of the last line illustrates the length and difficulty of the journey, implying the courage and heroism of battle, "my bleeding core" an image alluding as much to the violence of the inner transformations as to the grief of separation. The mood of the speaker, however, betrays his impatience and implies that God Himself may be holding back.

This suspicion of a deliberate delay is clearly voiced in this extract from another poem, one that portrays the divine Mother as the Godhead, which is more of an Eastern philosophical trope rather than the Western preferred Father figure:

> How long more shall I cry, Mother?
> How long shall I cry
> In a dark room alone, loving You?
> You know my secret thoughts,
> You know my heart's eagerness.

Why does dark death torture me every day?
How long will you delay, Mother?
How long will You delay?[26]

We have to ask now, what more does the Supreme demand of the seeker? What is the reason or the grounds for the Supreme to delay that final gift of the ultimate union? In this next poem is the portrayal of what can be viewed as a final step in the Trial series, the theme of temptation.

Love Is This, Also Love Is That

Love is the road that leads
Our souls to union vast.
Love is the passion-storm
That sports with our vital dust.

Love's child is emotion-flame.
Love's eyes are freedom, fear.
Love's heart is breath or death.
And love is cheap, love dear.[27]

Here we can find a contrast being set up between divine and human love, and the distinction is quite sharply delineated. The simple opening statement refers to love as the path to God-union, of each individual soul with its higher Source. However, the subsequent aspects of human love are drawn in a disjointed and more poignant way: the "passion-storm" of

---

[26] Extract from untitled poem by Sri Chinmoy, *The Garden of Love-Light,* p. 39.

[27] Sri Chinmoy, *My Flute,* p. 85.

love; the overwhelming nature of passionate human love, that "sports" or toys with our feelings – something that seems not only ephemeral, but out of control; and the highly suggestive use of the word "dust", evocative of the ruins or remains in the wake of a storm or fire.

The elaboration in the second stanza confirms this emerging unequivocal view by the poet that it is human love that emerges as deceptive, transient. "Love's child", the inevitable consequence is "emotion-flame", a mere chimera. Both impart images of immaturity, something that flares up intensely and dies out quickly like a passing childish tantrum. The enticing semantics following, "freedom, fear", juxtapose these contrary but simultaneous dispositions, and again "breath or death", intimate its risk and possessiveness, or fulfilment and denial. The final line seems to clinch this sobering delineation of love in the poem, the illusion that love can be bought and sold, not returned, or even discarded. The curtain is drawn back on the capriciousness and uncertainty of the human love relationship. And yet there is also a hint that divine love itself does not come too easily or too cheaply in the human quest for the ultimate love.

The need for human love is in many spiritual traditions the strongest and most trying "temptation"; we recall the Lord Christ's Temptation here. In the Quest it serves to avert the seeker's gaze from the highest goal, the final prize, and here we see its limitations. It is exposed as conditional, belonging to the physical world, tied to our life's limited breath and therefore destructive in its possessiveness compared to the eternal union to be found with the Divine. The throwaway last line refers us back to the slightly flippant note of the title. As a definition poem it recalls the technique of Emily Dickinson, who often plays with paradoxical images in her definition poems:

> Experience is the Angled Road
> Preferred against the Mind
> By–Paradox–the Mind itself–
> Presuming it to lead
>
> Quite Opposite–How Complicate
> The Discipline of Man–
> Compelling Him to Choose Himself
> His Preappointed Pain– [28]

Experience here is "Angled", alluding to both angular and tangential; as well as perhaps pre-ordained rather than thought out or planned by the mind, for the mind always believes itself to be sovereign. Dickinson illustrates here those grey areas of the mind, where the mind convinces itself it wants the opposite "pains" and perhaps we learn an unexpected lesson. Perhaps the final stanza intuits a definition of the law of *karma* as suggested in Eastern philosophy: that it is the soul that is really sovereign, and the soul that chooses. The experiences of life are, in fact, pre-ordained.

Although the following poem can be placed either before or after realisation in the Quest, I have used it here to interpret and characterize another temptation for the spiritual seeker, that of the call of the secular life.

---

[28] Thomas H. Johnson (ed.), *Final Harvest,* (No. 910), p. 219.

The Boat of Time Sails On

The sky calls me,
The wind calls me,
The moon and the stars call me.
The green and the dense groves call me,

The dance of the fountain calls me,
Smiles call me, tears call me.
A faint melody calls me.
The morn, noon and eve call me.

Everyone is searching for a playmate,
Everyone is calling me, "Come, come!"
One voice, one sound, all around.
Alas, the Boat of Time sails on.[29]

The charm of this piece lies in the repetitious structure of the fantastical call to come and play, from every corner of existence. The world with its myriad charms, even the seduction of humanity's endless joys and sorrows. All is animated with the inner light of consciousness itself and the allure is magical, for yes, we are all "searching for a playmate". However, it all melts into the speaker's conscious awareness of the unity, the oneness of existence and hence he is compelled to resist. The seeker's imperative is to disengage from the beauty of multiplicity so to speak, and recognize his own pressing duties in the face of time and the Goal in the Cosmic Game.

One final poem illustrates the dangers to be had in the temptation of settling for fulfilment in any one aspect of

[29] Sri Chinmoy, *My Flute,* p. 48.

existence available to the human spirit and again here we revisit the structure of our own inner hierarchy of being.

Vision-Skies

The body
Loves to be swayed by the wind of emotion.
The vital
Loves the prickings of desire.
The mind
Loves the confines of the finite.
The heart
Loves to be in the galaxy of saints.
The soul
Loves the life of unhorizoned vision-skies.[30]

The five-tiered hierarchy of the self, as Sri Chinmoy characterises it, is set up in such a way that a rhetorical question must silently be formed by the reader – who do I identify with here? Each part of the inner being seems to be struggling for supremacy; even the heart is shown to have its limitations, satisfied with "the galaxy of saints". The ever-striving and transcending nature of the soul shows the highest vision and the most perfect harmony to be achieved. Humanity's nobler aspirations, always declining to be confined, naturally gravitate towards the freedom of "unhorizoned vision-skies", the limitless nature of the soul. In the following Sri Chinmoy further explains his immeasurably profound insight into the mystical inner life of man and again implores us to open our eyes to the hidden meaning of life:

---

[30] Sri Chinmoy, *The Dance of Life*, p. 26.

> Deep inside us there are seven lower worlds and seven higher worlds. We are trying to transform the lower worlds into luminous worlds, worlds of perfection, and, at the same time, we are trying to bring the higher worlds into outer manifestation. Some of the higher worlds we already see operating in our physical world, on earth. First comes the physical, then the vital, then the mind, then the plane of intuition or the intuitive mind, then the overmind and the supermind. After the supermind comes Existence-Consciousness-Bliss – *Sat-Chit-Ananda.* If you know how to observe them, you can see that some of these worlds are already functioning in you.[31]

In reality, these lyrics can be seen as a series of vignettes of the inner life, each one the expression of a momentary intuition of far-reaching consequence, with not a little significance for Western understanding of spirituality. In Bradbury and McFarlane's work, the comment is made on Modernist lyrics that "are given by a slow underground process of psychic development, often only discernible in retrospect. To write a series of lyrics is more like keeping a spiritual diary than anything."[32] This seems an apt description of the lyrics of Sri Chinmoy.

In this chapter, the organization of the poetry has charted an inner journey of the individual spirit through trial, both apparent and concealed, while at the same time enlarging and illumining the scope of The Ever-Transcending Quest for the highest Consciousness. I feel the series as it is organized here, illustrates that the poetry has much more significance as a body of work than any single poem taken alone can reveal. The cumulative

[31] Sri Chinmoy, *Samadhi and Siddhi*, p. 8.

[32] Bradbury and McFarlane (eds.), *Modernism,* p. 320.

effects of the techniques of the poet, in such archaisms as rhetoric, repetition and revelation, work as a strong force compelling the reader to further investigation of the adventure of the Quest, and their own inner responses to the revelatory philosophical content.

As the reader follows the development of each step in the Quest, so he is called upon to make ever-deeper responses to the literary materials he is presented with. The literary materials themselves become more complex and demanding with each layer, especially in the next chapter, the Return, and, therefore, are more insistent upon a more complex response; a response that may entail challenging many previously hard-won ideas and beliefs. In any case the lyrics have such a compelling power that the re-assessment is often made surreptitiously, automatically, in the reading. As Barthes has observed, the reader is "a changing ensemble of social and aesthetic values, attitudes and forms of consciousness".[33]

Within the framework of the poetry of Sri Chinmoy, as Bennett notes, "In some poems, the effort of comprehension itself would seem to signify a kind of spiritual growth".[34] Of course in the mythology of the Quest, the archetypal hero must return home with some kind of treasure or transformation through knowledge that will in turn be of benefit to those around him. In the next and final chapter, Return, I will explore in the poetry the attainment of the goal of God-realisation or Self-realisation by Sri Chinmoy, the ultimate spiritual fulfilment, and what the poet indicates as its significance for all of humanity.

---

[33] Roland Champagne, *Literary History in the Wake of Roland Barthes*, p. 48.

[34] Bennett, op. cit., p. 47.

2. Sri Chinmoy meditating at an evening function, New York, August, 1995

3

The Return

THE PREVIOUS CHAPTER – the Trial – began an exploration of those steps that a spiritual aspirant must endure to break through obstacles and overcome human failings before union with his Beloved can be attained. Here, in this Chapter, we finally come to the poet's work which seeks to describe the experience of that Union. This is the culmination of the spiritual quest and through the final topics we witness how the English language, hewn by the divine Poet, portrays the exalted states of fulfilment and blissful absorption into divine Consciousness.

The Return encompasses the following topics:

- Unconditional surrender
- Attaining the Goal: God-Realisation/Self-Realisation
- Manifestation
- Beyond

As we all can recognize from our favourite stories, the archetypal protagonist in Quest mythology is frequently sent or compelled to venture on a journey, overcome trials of courage and endurance, win a treasure, secret knowledge or powers, and return with a new wisdom which will elevate him or her above the ordinary human being. In the ever-transcending spiritual quest portrayed in the writings of Sri Chinmoy, we can recognize many of the recurring motifs of quest mythology. These universal motifs may take on a deeply personal layer of significance as they resonate with our own individual quest for identity and purpose. They may even lead us to speculate on humanity's true hidden purpose and destiny. Indeed, we may ask if humanity's spiritual quest for its own inherent divinity is actually the archaic prototype for all quest traditions, stemming from past aeons; a deep unconscious aspiration for a lost unity, which is even now still unfolding.

In this chapter, I wish to show how Sri Chinmoy illustrates and documents his philosophy that the ultimate key to God-Realisation or Self-Realisation is an unconditional surrender to the Inner Pilot or the Will of the soul – that part of the *Self* that is in actual fact a tiny portion of the Absolute Consciousness. We have seen that the challenge is to distinguish that inner voice from the myriad of others clamouring for predominance – the mind, vital, physical and so on. The writings of Sri Chinmoy give us an exceptionally rare opportunity to explore the final attainment and expression of union with the highest consciousness, the true Self. In addition, through Sri Chinmoy's lyrics we can trace how he has approached and overcome the problem of using the medium of the English language to express this lofty state.

I believe that the oracy evidenced in much of the poetry of Sri Chinmoy arises from his ability to create pieces in entirety. Sri Chinmoy often wrote or dictated his work from a meditative state, explaining that he was simply engaged in "bringing down" the message from a higher realm. Across the span of time he was based in New York, some forty-three years, his poetry changed and became more free, economical and aphoristic in style. This gift, coupled with the almost timeless and sceneless nature of the verse, serves to highlight and emphasize the internal nature of the Quest. This in turn lends itself to the backdrop of the universal and frames the individual experience in epic dimensions.

In this first example, "Hope-Blossoms", we begin to see the spiritual aspirant coming to an understanding of the necessary steps towards unconditional surrender.

Hope-Blossoms

All my hopes will be blossomed like flowers
When I learn the language of surrender.
When I do not burn myself
In the fire of desire,
And when peace is desired by my restless mind,
Then my life will grow
Into the flower of beauty divine.[1]

In this brief lyric the poet suggests that surrender itself is a relatively foreign concept to humanity. Indeed, it is a subject as large as a new language, something that has to supplant the relentless reasoning of the mind and transcend the myriad wants of the life of desire. The image of blossoming flowers, yoked to the impulse of hope, inspires the imagination and contrasts starkly with oft-times destructive desires and the restlessness of human life: "When I do not burn myself/In the

---

[1] J.M. and H. Roberts (eds.), *Selected Poetry of Sri Chinmoy*, p. 60.

fire of desire". Temptation now has to be transcended by the seeker. This consuming image of self-immolation is in stark contrast to the surrender that moves us towards a state of peace for the restless mind. The seeker is poised momentarily between the ordinary struggles in life and the life of "beauty divine". It is clear that the restless mind and vital consciousness must of necessity join in the quest for the highest prize. However, it is not the indignity of a slave's surrender to a master that is envisaged; it has be understood that surrender entails a less developed part of the self-surrendering to the highest, most illumined part of the self. The sustaining image is that the poverty of human life will be supplanted. The seeker is growing into his divine nature, for as Sri Chinmoy frequently affirms: "God is our most illumined part. We cannot separate God from our existence."[2]

In the following poem, we witness how much the seeker is willing to sacrifice to attain surrender. As Whitman used the idea of flight to characterize the soul – "I fly the flight of the fluid and swallowing Soul" – Sri Chinmoy uses the metaphor of the soul as a bird in flight, in some inner sky, mimicking the feeling of the aspiration or upliftment of the heart in meditation:[3]

> Break asunder all my hopes.
> Only keep one hope,
> And that hope is to learn

---

[2] Sri Chinmoy, *Samadhi and Siddhi*, p. 23.

[3] Justin Kaplan (ed.), *Walt Whitman: Complete Poetry and Selected Prose*, p. 63.

The language of Your inner Silence
In my utter, unconditional surrender,
In Your clear and free Sky I shall be calm
And perfect.
The bird of my heart is dancing today
In the festival of supernal Light.[4]

The seeker's mood here seems one of desperation. He invokes God as Power, imploring God to sunder all, to sever even all the fragile human hopes of ambition, ego and ignorance that separate them. The small human notions of how we can aspire to reach God by our own efforts have been discarded. The phrase "utter, unconditional surrender", evokes an image of complete inner submission, almost annihilation, to achieve an absorption of the personality. It is a call for a complete separation from the ego. It brings to mind sacrifice, but again it is the sacrifice only of the lower nature, a divine transformation to reach a higher perfection. And with this relinquishment, the final boon of freedom can be attained. To be absorbed into the unknown "Silence", the clear and free sky of the Supreme Being, seems paradoxically both a terrifying and compelling prospect for the subject of the poem. Yet, we see the inner being rejoicing at the prospect of the prize and we join the jubilation: the final image of expectation anticipates a celebration of the Light "supernal".

It is worth digressing to a short definition poem that meditates upon the nature of "Silence", which Sri Chinmoy uses to profile the lofty realms of the Absolute Being.

---

4 Sri Chinmoy, *The Garden of Love-Light*, p. 46.

Silence Speaks, Silence Leads

Silence is not silent.
Silence speaks.
It speaks most eloquently.

Silence is not still.
Silence leads
It leads most perfectly.[5]

The poet plays on the idea of the silence of meditation not as an absence or emptiness, but rather as a substance, a benevolent communication, a movement. The term "eloquently" suggests a delicacy and mastery in the state of *nirvana*, the higher state of meditative fulfilment. This state is sometimes caricatured to the Western sensibility as static or comatose. For Sri Chinmoy, it is a state of wisdom, dynamic as well as ecstatic, more fecund and profound than we can envisage. Furthermore, this substantive silence has definite metaphysical qualities of intent, of leadership, inferring the eternally revealed truth, hence subtly revealing the omnipotent, omniscient Being who permeates all. It is interesting to note that Sri Chinmoy often uses the term "fulness" to describe that ineffable feeling of the Supreme inside us, a presence rather than an absence, satisfying, expansive and complete. This exposition of the "profile" or personality of the Divine is often drawn in delightful and surprising ways in the writings of Sri Chinmoy and will be revisited later.

In the next example, Sri Chinmoy plays further with the

---

[5] Sri Chinmoy, *Lord, Receive This Little Undying Cry*, p. 123.

paradoxical nature of the state of surrender for the speaker.

A Mystery

Whatever appears to leave us
Actually does not leave,
Whatever appears to stay with us
Actually does not stay,
Nothing remains.
Everything is a mystery
Of constant gain and loss.[6]

This is a restatement of the paradox in different ways; a contemplation, which illustrates the wonderment, bafflement, even amusement of the speaker. His deepening mystification over the state of being he is experiencing illustrates to us the shifting sands of the notion of the self. Impossible to paraphrase, one can only move around the peripheral intimations: the expected loss of individuality, freedom, limitation or even materiality itself, is actually reversed in surrender. The unreachable – liberation – is the prize won, yet is it actually only rediscovered? This poem strongly evokes the ineffability and unknowability of the divine Will and purpose, particularly in relation to surrender.

The metaphor of life as a sea journey is a thread in literature that comes down to us from ancient times, employed by writers ranging from the Stoics, through to the Transcendentalist tradition and into the modern era. It is also utilized extensively by Sri Chinmoy, who portrays the Supreme Consciousness or

---

[6] J.M. and H. Roberts, op. cit., p. 59.

God, as a Boatman, steering the seeker towards the Goal. Walt Whitman also uses this metaphor, portraying the "cheerful boatmen" rowing across time. It is as much a metaphor perhaps for the lives that have gone before, hinting at cycles of evolution:

> Immense have been the preparations for me . . .
> Cycles ferried my cradle, rowing and rowing like cheerful boatmen.[7]

In the following poem, Sri Chinmoy extends the metaphor.

O My Boatman

O my Boat, O my Boatman,
O message of Transcendental Delight,
Carry me. My heart is thirsty and hungry,
And it is fast asleep at the same time.
Carry my heart to the other shore.
The dance of death I see all around
The thunder of destruction indomitable I hear.
O my Inner Pilot, You are mine,
You are the Ocean of Compassion infinite.
In You I lose myself,
My all in You I lose.[8]

The metaphor of the sea journey for Sri Chinmoy perfectly encapsulates the human spiritual quest. The Supreme Being is the boat, the vessel, as well as the Boatman, the Inner Pilot inside man and the destination, the Goal itself. The "other shore" is that haven where the heart will be fulfilled

[7] J.M. and H. Roberts, op. cit., p. 80.

[8] Sri Chinmoy, *My Flute*, p. 60.

at last. All these images are blended into one to symbolize the "Ocean of Compassion infinite". The Supreme Consciousness is not only permeating all, it is All. As the seeker finally becomes aware of this sublime ocean of Consciousness, he partakes of an interaction, the gift of divine Compassion. Thus, he escapes the disintegration and entropy of the death-in-life dance of the ordinary, the mundane and potentially destructive world. The self, which had been trapped in a repetitious dance of forgetfulness in death and forced to begin the journey to self-consciousness again after each re-birth, is finally absolved. The restatement at the close is a dual affirmation for the surrender of the capacities and the ego of the seeker, and the subsequent assimilation of man into God.

The following poem also suggests that the descent of Compassion is an integral part of the interchange between the seeker and the divine, but, by contrast with the dramatic portrayal in the former piece, this is a more tender and intimate portrait.

Tumi amai diyechho aj samarpaner bani
Ami tomai sanpechhi mor kusum hriday khani
Andhar rate ashru sathe
Moher karar ajanate
Simar gehe thakbona ar jani ami jani
Tumi amar jenechhi ma chirantaner rani

The Message of Surrender

Today You have given me
The message of surrender.

I have offered to You
My very flower-heart.
In the dark night with tears,
In the unknown prison-cell of illusion,
In the house of the finite,
No longer shall I abide.
I know You are mine.
I have known this, Mother,
O Queen of the Eternal.[9]

In this example, we see the poet using the characteristic Eastern invocation of God as the Mother, with its context of the sweetness and intimacy between mother and child. It becomes apparent here that the "message of surrender" has originated with the divine as a form of Grace that is bestowed upon the seeker. The lines "In the dark night with tears/In the unknown prison-cell of illusion/In the house of the finite" not only signify the world of human suffering and limited vision, but also the suffering that ensues for the individual seeker in his separate physical form, apart from the divine. The prison-cell of illusion alludes to the *maya,* the deception of the physical world, whereas the "house of the finite" describes the frailty and brief mortality of the human body. The Mother, the "Queen of the Eternal", in Her divine aspect of Compassion has showered Her blessings in the form of surrender itself. It is She who has wrought this miracle, bestowed the message that guides the way. The hard-won realisation is understood, "I know You are mine", and yet again there is that sense that

---

[9] Sri Chinmoy, *My Flute*, p. 89.

this was always known at some level. Once more we witness the paradoxical exchange, that it is the Supreme who will bestow the surrender before the self can be offered and before the divine in turn can be felt, realised and regained.

This exchange of capacities between the Mother and child, the Divine and human, is an intrinsic feature of the philosophy of Sri Chinmoy, emphasizing in turn the equality and interdependence of both. It is this perfect, selfless love and trust between the parent and child that is held up as the emblem of the divine relationship. This simple reality, perhaps eternally known, recalled and revealed, is not only attainable by all, but inevitable, as Sri Chinmoy takes great pains to assure us over and again.

Two Hopes of God

Two hopes of God:
Man will take His place,
Man will give Him rest,
Eternity's rest.[10]

The next step in the Quest is the ultimate one, the pinnacle of spiritual and mystical experience. It is the expression of realisation itself. In the following series of lyrics Sri Chinmoy invites the reader to witness the culmination of the seeker's journey. The Goal is at last irrevocably won and the reader can stand with the poet on the verge of this revelation as he attempts to express the inconceivable beauty of this, the highest spiritual union. As Bennett has noted previously, any expression

---

[10] Sri Chinmoy, *When God-Love Descends*, p. 43.

here must remain a severe understatement of the actual experience of God-union. Sri Chinmoy joins his forebears from many mystical and literary traditions who have dared to "point a finger at the moon". His style and poetic technique have been noted by critics to have much in common with the language of Krishna's teachings in *Bhagavad-Gita*, tones possessed of the same certainty and emphatic authority that are found in the traditions of Indian "wisdom" literature.[11] The enchanting appeal, power and beauty of the lyrics of Sri Chinmoy are heightened by the deliberate understatement and the poetic techniques employed.

Beyond Speech and Mind

Beyond speech and mind,
Into the river of ever-effulgent Light
My heart dives.
Today thousands of doors,
Closed for millennia,
Are opened wide.[12]

The imagery here is carefully controlled; the jubilation understated; the emotion kept just below the surface. However, the words themselves seem to speak out with an explosive power on the vastness of the experience. The first line pushes against our intellect. Then "Into the river of ever-effulgent Light" we tumble, rushing headlong over the words as though caught in the current ourselves. In the intensity of that leap of the entire being, we have a sense of falling, diving, becoming

[11] Bennett, op. cit. ch. 3, p. 118.

[12] J.M. and H. Roberts, op. cit., p. 1.

immersed in the incandescent fluidity. Then a change of speed and tone arrests us briefly as this breathtaking accomplishment is surveyed, and we stand open-mouthed and speechless at the implications. "Today" echoes through thousands of doors; the knowledge of millennia is before us.

The quiet power of this imagery is evident from the implied "Infinity" opening up before us. We are dazzled by the characterization of the Supreme Consciousness inferred here by the radiance of "ever-effulgent Light". It is an image of heroic and divine proportions, and yet the extraordinary impression to be found at the close of this mighty achievement is one of humility. The speaker steps back and disappears, leaving the reader to partake of the achievement, the quiet elation of man standing on the threshold of eternal revelation, of aeons spread before him as a feast. Although this language appears clear and simple, the ideas are densely concentrated and philosophically evocative. Many of the previous steps in The Ever-Transcending Quest are implied and the poet conveys the experience as the culmination of a long, intricate process of evolution, both personal and universal.

In the following poem, Sri Chinmoy has used a more formal metrical structure, alternating four and five-foot iambic lines, thereby enhancing the gravitas.

Revelation

No more my heart shall sob or grieve.
My days and nights dissolve in God's own Light.
Above the toil of life my soul
Is a Bird of Fire winging the Infinite.

I have known the One and His secret Play,
And passed beyond the sea of Ignorance-Dream.
In tune with Him, I sport and sing;
I own the golden Eye of the Supreme.

Drunk deep of Immortality,
I am the root and boughs of a teeming vast.
My Form I have known and realised.
The Supreme and I are one; all we outlast.[13]

The speaker's tone, formalized and elevated here by the metre, begins to enter the realm of the heroic dimension of human experience. The mantric nature of the verse thrums like a heartbeat from the very first line. With its short syllables and chanting pace, it assumes a weight of majestic authority throughout. Impetus is added with the image of the "Bird of Fire" elevating the reader suddenly with the movement of flight, of unconstrained speed and freedom. The stark beauty and majesty of the image lights the imagination. The entire impression of the uplifting movement seems to inspire a corresponding feeling in the reader. In the second stanza the union with God is established as an experience of Oneness; being absorbed into the Light. The single "Eye of the Supreme" infers that the third eye, the eye of knowledge is now open. This image recalls the words of the Lord Christ that "the Light of Your Eye" shall flood the entire body with divine Light.

The timing and rhythm, the slower four-foot line, and then the faster pace of the five-foot line, create an elegant tension

[13] Sri Chinmoy, *My Flute*, p. 47.

that is highly suggestive of the ability now gained of stepping back and forth between the finite human and the infinite divine perspective of the theme. Specific images work powerfully to evoke the scope of the spiritual quest: the "secret play", God's "Game of Life"; "Ignorance-Dream" recalling the buffeting sea of human illusion in which we dwell. The fluctuating rhythm in the final line of each stanza with its pause and trochaic substitution have the effect of arresting our attention so that we may appreciate the enormity of the achievement being surveyed. The opening of the final stanza gives a strong impression of the immensity of feeling, a reeling as of drunkenness, whereas the following line indicates the metaphor of man as a tree, both of the earth and yet capable of stretching upward into an unknown sky, the "teeming vast", again emphasizing that outward, expanding notion of higher realms.

There is a sense of completion in the final line, the quiet and simple statement of the significance of the mortal human consciousness attaining the Immortal. It is not attaining God the Power that is being celebrated, but the enduring nature of God the Supreme Player in His own Cosmic Game.

The following poem is another example of the paradoxical wordplay Sri Chinmoy uses to explore the idea of union with the Divine.

> O Supreme, my Father-Son,
> Now that we two are one
> And won by each other won,
> Nothing remains undone.[14]

---

[14] Alan Spence (ed.), *Between Nothingness and Eternity*, p. 60.

This poem marries spiritual ideas from two great traditions: the idea from the Upanishads of the lover and the Beloved, the knower and the Known as interchangeable; as well as the Christian allusion to the Father-God and the Christ-Son being one entity. Sri Chinmoy's lyrics often do this so effortlessly, bridging philosophical divides and illuminating the underlying truths of universal spiritual dimensions. As described by Bennett, the combination of rhyme and rhetorical wordplay in this poem mirrors the experience of envelopment, "Its completeness is unassailable . . . theirs is a mutual inhabitation".[15]

The following poem also gives us a glimpse of existence in that higher realm:

Ami gahi gan tumi gaha bale
Tumi haso bale hasi
Banshari bajao hriday gabhire
Taito hayechhi banshi
Tumi je amar ami je tomar
Ei mor parichoy
Eka dhare tumi janaka janani
Chinmoyi Chinmoy

I Sing Because You Sing

I sing because You sing.
I smile because You smile.
Because You play on the flute
I have become Your flute.

[15] Bennett, op. cit., pp. 106ff.

You play in the depths of my heart.
You are mine, I am Yours.
This is my sole identification.
In one Form You are my Mother
    And Father eternal,
And Consciousness-moon, Consciousness-sun
    All pervading.[16]

The union of God-Realisation is characterized here by overlapping images of song, then of smile, each state of the Supreme calling up a similar ecstatic response in the speaker. The imagery alludes to portraits of Lord Krishna playing upon his flute. God is portrayed as the Supreme Musician and the poet/seeker as the instrument in order to illustrate the idea of total surrender to the Will of God. However, the image is also suggestive of children both playing with innocent delight. The poem moves from delightful praise of a personal Companion-God, through the intimacy of identification and then to a contemplation of the infinite aspects of the Divine Being, as Father in the West, Mother in the East, containing the dualities of stillness and action, purity and dynamism, justice and compassion. The rhythm accompanies the theme by opening with quite lively, short, stressed lines, gradually entering longer and more intricate patterns until the final line stretches into an endless, mesmerizing syllabic structure – "Consciousness-moon . . . All pervading". It is a stunning completion and we are left with the impression of sound ringing across the solar system or light expanding as the speaker relinquishes all identity to become

[16] J.M. and H. Roberts, op. cit., p. 41.

the child of Light.

The following poem, "The Absolute", is one of Sri Chinmoy's most celebrated expressions of the mystical union with God.

The Absolute

No mind, no form, I only exist;
    Now ceased all will and thought;
The final end of Nature's dance,
    I am It whom I have sought.

A realm of Bliss bare, ultimate;
    Beyond both knower and known;
A rest immense I enjoy at last;
    I face the One alone.

I have crossed the secret ways of life,
    I have become the Goal.
The Truth immutable is revealed;
    I am the way, the God-Soul.

My spirit aware of all the heights,
    I am mute in the core of the Sun.
I barter nothing with time and deeds;
    My cosmic play is done.[17]

Alternating four and three-foot iambic lines, rhyming *abcb*, give a measured sense of completion and solidity of form. Again, the extraordinarily stark impact of the lack of personality, allied with a sense of ubiquitous "presence" is everywhere apparent,

[17] Alan Spence, op. cit., p. 62.

giving the poem an acute euphonic cohesion. When a reader enters into the poem by reading it aloud, the oratorical impact is majestic. Bennett suggested that the rhetorical mode may well be man's natural choice of speech under certain spiritual stresses or conditions.[18] It is evident that the integrity of form here is perfectly in harmony with such absolute terms – "realm of Bliss", "Truth Immutable". The exultation and triumphant tones are held in balance by the simplicity of statements: "I face the One alone / . . . I have become the Goal". The profound assertion "I am the way, the God-Soul" brings dramatically to mind the spiritual achievements of other Masters. It is striking in its artless sincerity, revealing to us an entirely revolutionary possibility, that this state is indeed attainable in our lifetime, and in such a way that we witness the inherent realisation through eyes of both awe and humility.

A reconciliation of the small "I", the ego, which has been held suspended in the opening lines, purified, illumined and divinized, then melts into the ultimate image of fusion in the final stanza: "mute in the core of the Sun". In this simple designation of the absolute state of Eternal Consciousness, the self has been extended into pure Being, and the final lines emphasize that the wealth of time and eternity, mortality and immortality, the finite and the Infinite have been integrated. There is no further need for speech, no more bartering with karmic consequences, "time and deeds"; the end-game, the cosmic game has been resolved forthwith. The force and profound assurance of the speaking voice which here stems from the tones of incantation inherent in the formalized

[18] Bennett, op. cit., p. 8.

grammar and syntax is irresistible. The peace and ecstasy of the heights of God-union are merely hinted at by the imagery and sounds of the internal rhyme: "A realm of Bliss, bare, ultimate. . . . A rest immense I enjoy at last." We are invited to finally witness and contemplate the mysteries of life laid bare.

In discussing "The Absolute", Alan Spence commented that "poetry described as 'mantric' actually evokes the qualities it describes", and he goes on to relate the experience of a Scottish writer, Tom McGrath, while reciting this poem. The writer was attempting to illustrate the failure of English to express a "peculiarly Indian sensibility". He was subsequently shocked to observe the exact opposite result of the experiment:

> The words sprang from my lips and sounded in the room with an authority that was awe-inspiring. It became clear that we were listening to a voice speaking from the absolute pinnacle of human experience, and speaking *directly from it.* By the time we reached the closing lines, we were both dumbfounded. Not only had we heard a great poem, but we both felt we had been in the presence of a consciousness the nature of which filled us with the deepest humility and reverence.[19]

Again it is a profound example of how the lyrics of Sri Chinmoy can affect the reader, enlarging our comprehension of what is possible, drawing us up into the experience of the higher consciousness ourselves.

Of the Transcendentalists, I feel it is Thoreau, the self-confessed "mystic, transcendentalist and philosopher" who best understands the seeker striving for union with God as our destiny, and its implications:

---

[19] Alan Spence, op. cit., p. 9.

Then idle Time ran gadding by
And left me with Eternity alone;
I hear beyond the range of sound,
I see beyond the verse of sight, –
I see, smell, taste, hear, feel, that everlasting
Something to which we are allied,
    at once our maker, our abode,
    our destiny, our very Selves; . . . .
It doth expand my privacies
To all, and leave me single in the crowd.[20]

Thoreau is sensible of the Oneness of being, the inner worlds beyond and the promise of union with that eternal consciousness, in such a poignant way that places him alone in his time, yet he knows his limitations, the distance he has yet to cover in the journey:

> I would give all the wealth of the world, and all the deeds of all the heroes, for one true vision. But how can I communicate with the gods who am a pencil-maker on the earth, and not be insane?[21]

The receptivity of the Transcendendalists in the nineteenth century was remarkable. They positioned themselves outside religious restrictions and sought to break down the narrowness of their era. It would be interesting to surmise whether this was a necessary step in the evolution of the collective consciousness of America for, after all, it is the supreme Consciousness that is evolving in and through the human. Those

---

[20] Henry David Thoreau, *A Week on the Concord and Merrimack Rivers*, Penguin 1998, p. 139.

[21] H.D. Thoreau, op. cit., p. 112.

who came later and attempted to "place" them in religious contexts were perhaps missing the point. Although we are speaking here of an experience that goes beyond intellect, even beyond being classified as religious, it also seems too dismissive to relegate it to the "metaphysical".

Whilst the Transcendentalists were effectively beginning to break down the restrictive barriers of religion, Sri Chinmoy has gone beyond such barriers. His knowledge demands that we see the advent of the higher consciousness in our lives as completely practical, inevitable, and, in fact the opposite, its suppression as negligence or even a kind of madness! What becomes clear from this point is that there need never again be any intermediary standing between Lord Krishna and his *sannyasin*, Lord Buddha and his devotees, Lord Christ and his followers. We simply need to own and claim that Bird of Light, the Inner Pilot in our own breast.

As I mentioned at the outset, I have imposed my framework of the Quest, the Separation, the Trial and Return upon the writings of Sri Chinmoy for my own purposes. What will be most astonishing to understand now is that we must turn this entire journey of the Quest so far, on its head! The steps of The Ever-Transcending Quest in the poetry of Sri Chinmoy have been a useful device to illustrate the journey of life toward enlightenment for the seeker and as a kind of blueprint for humanity. However, it must be stated that the poems were not written in this order. In fact, Sri Chinmoy wrote many of these, the highest of his God-Realisation poems, as a very young man in the Sri Aurobindo Ashram in Pondicherry, India.

Sri Chinmoy recounts in his writings that he was no more than a youth when he regained his occult powers and knowledge of previous spiritual incarnations. In July 1944, at the age of twelve, after both his parents had passed away, he entered the Sri Aurobindo Ashram, and at the tender age of thirteen achieved the heights of his God-Realisation.[22] He explained his early experiences were like "revising a book" that he once knew very well. He recounts many stories from his teenage years: his vision of the cosmic goddess Sarasvati who came to him and played her *vina*, then smashed it to pieces and threw them into him, signifying that she had given him her musical abilities. Another recounts his story of "the Lord of my own heart" emerging from his heart as a breathtakingly beautiful, luminous golden boy, to speak with him. Another tells of the cosmic god Agni, his magnificent golden appearance and form and how it changes due to the way people perceive him; and of Agni's power, compassion and significance in the world.

Here is an extract from his account of an experience at the age of fourteen:

> Whenever I had the opportunity, I flew to the edge of the ever-blue sea and took my seat there in solitude. My bird of consciousness, dancing slowly, rose to the sky and lost itself up there. . . . I drank deeply of Ambrosia and was floating on an illumined ocean. It seemed that I no longer existed on this earth.

However, he explains, something suddenly put an end to this

---

[22] Sri Chinmoy, *Astrology, the Supernatural and the Beyond*, Aum Pubs., 1991, p. 7.

experience, and he began to feel it was all a useless childish dream and he could not even go on with life, when:

> A sudden flash of lightning appeared over my head. Looking up with awe and bewilderment, I found above me my Beloved, the King of the Universe looking at me. His radiant face was overcast with sorrow. "Father," I asked, approaching him, "what makes Thy Face so sad?"
>
> How can I be happy, My son, if you do not wish to be My companion and help Me in My Mission? I have, concealed in the world, millions of sweet plans which I shall unravel. If My children do not help Me in My Play, how can I have My Divine Manifestation here on earth? Profoundly moved, I bowed and promised: "Father, I will be Thy faithful companion, loving and sincere, throughout Eternity. Shape me and make me worthy of my part in Thy Cosmic Play and Thy Divine Mission."[23]

It could be regarded as well nigh impossible to assess either the spiritual achievements or other accomplishments of such a figure as Sri Chinmoy, unless one has the same height of spiritual accomplishment and awareness. Nevertheless, the maturity is evident for all to see and feel in the poetry. Later of course the simplicity and sincerity are evident as well in his illumining talks and lectures, plays and stories which all serve to guide us back into the heart consciousness. Reproduced below is the earliest known draft of "The Absolute", written around the age of 25 years, and almost exactly corresponding to the final version that he published in New York in 1972:

---

[23] Sri Chinmoy, *Awakening*, 1988, Scotland: Citadel Books, p. 49.

No mind, no form, I only exist;
Now ceased all will and thought.
A final end of Nature's dance
I am It whom I have sought.

A realm of bliss ultimate, bare;
Beyond both knower and known.
A rest immense I enjoy at last;
I face the One, alone.

I have known the secret ways of life,
I have become god-soul.
The Truth immutable is revealed
I am the way, the goal.

My spirit aware of all the heights,
I am mute in the core of Sun.
I barter nothing with time and deeds
My cosmic play is done.

So few changes! It was not necessary for Sri Chinmoy to work and rework over his drafts. It would be reasonable to assume that the transcendental accomplishment of Sri Chinmoy, as found in his lyrics and other writings, stops here at the highest achievement. After all, the "Goal is won", the God-Realisation attained, and his "play" he claims is done. Is this not the point at which the Master removes himself from the real world and becomes a recluse? Sri Chinmoy received an inner command from his Beloved to go to the West at 32 years of age, after spending twenty years serving his spiritual community, writing and deepening his spiritual achievement. This would have been no small undertaking for one who had spent almost his entire life in a sheltered spiritual community. Obediently he accepted this directive from his Inner Pilot. This "little Indian village boy", as he called himself, began an extraordinary adventure in one of the most intense and cosmopolitan of modern cities, New York, in 1964.

Baffled at first by the West, he took the guidance of his Inner Pilot at every step. And these steps led to his life's work, the manifestation of his light and realisation. It was an extraordinary mission. He simply began by pouring his light out into the world. His Inner Pilot inspired him to fill every waking moment with writing, painting, composing music, entering the physical world of sport, travelling to every corner of the globe to meditate with those who felt inspired by his presence. He became, in effect, a divine ambassador.

Never ceasing to write poetry, Sri Chinmoy expressed the manifestation of his achievement in such a myriad of ways and so profusely it will no doubt confound future generations. His comment to the critics was that quantity and quality were both necessary. He developed and extended his talents into many and diverse activities, both as an inspiration to humanity to transcend its limitations by tapping into the hidden power of the inner life and as a way of making concrete the higher spiritual realities.

In his poetry, we can discern and follow this imperative to illustrate and articulate the Supreme's Will through the now perfected human instrument:

Where

Where Peace once sang
I became my Father's flowing Grace.

Where Love once sang
I became my Father's glowing Face.

Where Truth once sang
I became my Father's master Race.[24]

The poet is here beginning to reflect on the end result of his realisation – the miracle of the achievement of the highest knowledge. He uses a semantic and phonetic paradigm to elaborate on the very complex transformations that have taken place on the spiritual level to illustrate his multi-level experience. The analysis of the lyrics is difficult: the poem is enigmatic, indeed. We can try to ponder the possibilities: is it that the speaker was first the recipient, and then becomes the bestower of divine peace, love and truth?

S.R. Levin may offer a guide to poetic analysis in this instance: "the poem generates its own code, of which the poem is the only message – the syntagms generate particular paradigms and these paradigms in turn generate the syntagms in this way leading us back into the poem."[25] Perhaps the best response we can make, and the instinctive one, is to respond with the heart.

It is with that quiet voice, confident, assertive, that Sri

---

[24] Sri Chinmoy, *My Flute*, p. 51.

[25] S.R. Levin, *Linguistic Structures in Poetry*, p. 41.

Chinmoy gently states the paradox that the human and the Divine are one and explores the inevitability of this destiny for humanity. If we revisit the idea of the quest, where the traditional hero must return to society with some kind of benefit or prize, it is easy to equate this with what Sri Chinmoy terms "the fruits of realisation". Often he stated that some seekers manage to touch the tree, others climb up to the top of the tree, and still others climb down again to share the fruits with humanity. The latter is what he calls "manifestation". It is possible that no other Master has spent so long and worked so arduously to establish such a permanent imprint of this higher light.

One of Sri Chinmoy's significant aims through his creative expressions is to provide instruction for his disciples. Sri Chinmoy's extensive writing; 22,000 mantric songs; and many thousands of paintings, which can be used as *mandala*s for concentration and meditation. Taken as a whole, they detail every step of the seeker's journey and map the realm of inner experiences. In addition, extensive question and answer series have been published which cover a vast range of topics from the highest spiritual perspective. His major volumes of poetry include the *Ten Thousand Flower-Flames* series and *Twenty-Seven Thousand Aspiration-Plants*. Much later in life, Sri Chinmoy began the *Seventy-Seven Thousand Service-Trees*. Targeted towards the *sadhana* (discipline/practice) of the spiritual aspirant, many of these poems fall into the classifications of the rhetorical modes: "Docere", "Delectare" and "Movere" (to teach, to delight, to move). Sri Chinmoy was able to fully identify with the hearts and minds of his students, and every joy and sorrow, triumph and failure they experienced along the way. In return, he offered his inner strength and wisdom:

> If you have a disturbing thought,
> Then come to me.
> I shall give you my challenging will.
>
> If you have an impure mind,
> Then come to me.
> I shall give you my pure heart.
>
> If you have an uncomely body,
> Then come to me.
> I shall give you my beautiful soul.
>
> If you have an unsatisfied life,
> Then come to me.
> I shall give you my satisfied God.[26]

This poem appeals on a deep and personal level to the *dis-ease* of our modern life: our disturbed thoughts often arising from the daily bombardment of our mind with worldly impurities, or our constant clamouring for distraction, for satisfaction. They are contrasted with the strength and dignity of the poet's promise: "I shall give you. . . . " The reader is reassured by his measured and honest offering of solace, refuge and succour. It is the tendency for a downward inflexion at the end of each second and third line, mirroring the rhythm of ordinary speech and repetition that gives this poem a tone of quiet assurance, confidentiality and deliverance. Here then is our sanctuary and a means to our own peace and fulfilment.

---

[26] Sri Chinmoy, *Meditation: Man-Perfection in God-Satisfaction*, p. 2.

We have a direct sense that these are not inflated promises, an instant fix, nor are they for everyone indiscriminately. The emphasis is always on the subordinating conjunction "If", the supposition that there are some who find life wanting. Humility shines through the choice of expression. We are encouraged to open our eyes to what it is possible to receive from a Self-realised master, the God-representative who is accessible if we so choose. Our lasting impression is of a "satisfied God", an appealing but also revolutionary notion for us to consider, as we have often been taught to view God as one who finds us wanting.

Sri Chinmoy often displays great humour and sometimes irony in his expression of the dilemmas and paradoxes facing the spiritual teacher, largely because such a personage can be so often misunderstood or dismissed in the world. This is one such example:

Although

Although I teach, I am the cap of fools;
Although I love all souls, a fiend am I.
I am not strong, yet for the weak I fight;
At will I sell myself and myself I buy.

At every pause my life I contradict.
To me are ever the same all truths and lies.
To me the earthly beings and He are one.
We fly in His Bosom vast, in us He flies.[27]

This poetic meditation on the dilemmas facing the master of spiritual attainment begins with a lighthearted lament and then

---

[27] Sri Chinmoy, *My Flute*, p. 75.

builds towards a contemplation of the inevitable interdependence of the human and the divine. There is a weight and even-tempered nature to the paradox, emphasized and echoed by the even break of the caesura in each line, and the cadence of the speech. It is impossible to paraphrase effectively, yet like Sisyphus we are impelled to try: is this the teacher's stance when he knows that he will be ignored, misunderstood, even derided? Is this lover of souls also one who must be detached to become the taskmaster? Or, is he the one dispensing compassion on behalf of the Supreme, the barterer, for recognition and publicity for *The* most Renowned of all Beings? Or, is this the bartering of the seeker's ignorance for the illumined light of the master?

In the second stanza, we find the one who envisions *karma* which simply put means action, or the equivalent of our "truths and lies", sees our fate as inevitable and necessary because the real "actor" in us is the Supreme Himself. And we are left once again with that final image of the interconnectedness of existence, the symbiosis of man and God. This poem is brimming with spiritual nuances inherent in the position of the master who undertakes to teach and try to make the Supreme Consciousness manifest in a world that is so unaware and ignorant of the workings of the inner divinity in life. We can only commiserate with such self-mockery!

Again it brings to mind Emily Dickinson who also dilates on the paradoxical nature of the Oneness of reality in her work: "One and One – are One – / Two be finished using. . . . "[28] In

[28] Emily Dickinson, *Final Harvest*, No. 314, p. 191.

the poem below, she indicates the reciprocity of the effort:

Each–its difficult Ideal
Must achieve–Itself–
Through the solitary prowess
Of Silent Life–[29]

Dickinson shares with Sri Chinmoy an intensity in brevity. They both have a unique style which lends itself to the expression of the transcendental. On occasion, however, Sri Chinmoy extends our comprehension into something more encompassing, our own personal quest, challenging us and gently guiding us to consider and experience the level of the heart consciousness. His poem becomes an instructional tool for the illustration of our own divinity. Often he indicates that we stand on the brink of a new Golden Age, a time when man will recognize his equal standing as a partner of God in His highest Aspect.

Here is an example of Sri Chinmoy as the seer-poet illustrating the significance of the twenty-first century in the evolution of humanity, taken from his book *The New Millennium*:

The fulfillment of the mind
Has been the hope
Of the past few centuries.
Now the fulfillment of the heart
Will be the hope
Of the next generation

[29] Inder Kher, *The Landscape of Absence: Emily Dickinson's Poetry*, From No. 750, p. 75.

And of all generations to come.
Indeed, this will be a unique
Contribution
Of the 21st Century to humanity.[30]

I believe this tendency in the writings of Sri Chinmoy is unique and of revolutionary significance for both the interpretation of the past as well as preparation for a future.

I have aspired to show how poems of manifestation move towards the unveiling of the equality and interdependence of the Supreme Consciousness within the physical world. However, there are entire categories of poems which move beyond this stage, illustrating the ever Self-transcending nature of the Supreme Being Himself, not only in and through the creation, but within His own Transcendental "Dream". Here is an amusing example, which gives insight into the Divinity having a healthy sense of humour:

Tomorrow's Supreme Surprise

Yesterday's supreme surprise:
Today I shall realise God.
Today's supreme surprise:
Tomorrow I shall become another God.
Tomorrow's supreme surprise:
The day after tomorrow I shall resign
And give back to my predecessor
His post,

[30] Sri Chinmoy, *The New Millennium*, New York: Agni Press, 1999, p. 50.

His responsibility,
His headache.[31]

Sri Chinmoy comments:

> Human consciousness is limited, earthbound; it gets joy in the finite. Divine consciousness wants to expand constantly . . . always an ever self-transcending goal because God is constantly transcending Himself. Even though He is limitless, He is also making progress.[32]

One fascinating aspect of Sri Chinmoy's prolific outpouring which is worthy of note is the wonderful characterization of his relationship with the Divine Being, his Beloved Supreme, through what may be termed "conversation" poems. There is a diverse array of these poems sprinkled throughout his work. They are intimate exchanges, glimpses into a higher perspective. They may portray conversations between the seeker and God, the son and Father, the daughter and the Supreme. There are even some which consist of questions and answers between the *yogi* and the entity of death. These pieces have a fascination, a charm and enchantment of their own which is difficult to ignore due to the perceived impossibility of a human being ever partaking of such encounters. They seem to draw back the curtain of eternity, infinity and immortality to give us a rare glimpse of that higher realm of being. They make us step back thoughtfully in appreciation and contemplation of this higher point of view, and reconsider our own assumptions and certitudes about life. Most often in the question and answer formats they display a language of authority, and tonal

[31] Sri Chinmoy, *Europe-Blossoms*, p. 484.

[32] Sri Chinmoy, *Samadhi and Siddhi*, p. 1.

amplitude to reveal a fascinating sense of the personality of God.

"My Lord, I am singing."
"Fine, that is what pleases Me."
"My Lord, I am dancing."
"Wonderful, that is what enchants Me."
"My Lord, I am suffering."
"No, My child, you are not suffering.
That is not true.
What is happening is that you
are having a series of experiences.
Furthermore, try to realise that it is I
who am having all the experiences
in and through you."

"My Lord, is there anything sweeter than forgiveness?"
"Yes, My child, gratitude is by far sweeter than forgiveness."
"My Lord, is there anything more fulfilling than the feeling of oneness?"
"Yes, My child, when you feel that you are the Eternal Lover and I am your Eternal Beloved, and when you feel that I am the Eternal Lover and you are My Eternal Beloved, the feeling of oneness is supremely transcended and immortally fulfilled."

"My Lord, I know that You don't have to read any books. Nevertheless, have You read a few books, or should I say any books?"
"My child, I have read only three books in all My endless Life.

The first book I read is called Life, written by your mother, Infinity,
The second book is called Realisation, written by My son, Eternity.
The third book is called Manifestation, written by My daughter Immortality."[33]

The interaction here is not a simple creative device or contrivance. It is, in fact, an articulation, a record of an exchange. The divine Entity is revealed in an exchange replete with ease of intimacy, with simplicity and authority. The persona thus expressed holds within it an unmistakable stamp of authenticity. We are brought up short with the explication of a divine Will that, it is claimed, can never be fathomed or understood. Yet, with some surprise, we have to admit it cannot be easily refuted.

Lord, I seek and You hide.
I seek because without You
My life-flames do not and cannot burn.
Now Lord, tell me,
Why do You hide?

"Daughter, I hide because
My hiding intensifies your seeking.
It gratifies your loving,
Glorifies your achievement
And immortalises your enlightenment."

---

[33] Sri Chinmoy, *God's Secrets Revealed*, New York: Herder & Herder, 1971, pp. 45, 81, 84.

My Lord, is there any time
When You do not love me?
"Yes, My child, there is a time."
When, my Lord, when?
"When you think that you are not
A budding God."[34]

We find a purity, plausibility and authority embedded in the play of language between the speakers, validating and explicating eternal truths, and yet gently mocking of humanity's foibles. The charm and enduring patience of the divine voice are difficult to ignore, promoting understanding, even sympathy for the Supreme's point of view. It evokes, inevitably, an awakening within us at a very deep level, one that must reject outmoded caricatures of a demanding deity and with relief welcome new ideas of an intimate and accessible friend. Again, when read in the context of Sri Chinmoy's larger body of work, it entices us to explore and synthesize these inner and higher worlds, expanding our own point of view.

As the writing style of Sri Chinmoy developed, his poetry became more concise, aphoristic and mantric in quality. Sri Chinmoy mentioned many times that at first, upon adopting the English language, he felt it could never embody sacred *mantra* in the same way as Sanskrit or his native Bengali. However, in time he changed his mind. He realised that all languages could be bent towards the sacred mantric quality that he desired. His lyrics became shorter, and yet still retained

[34] Sri Chinmoy, *God Is – Selected Writings*, New York: Aum Publications, 1997, pp. 11, 25.

that epic breadth of the poet who stands at both the foot of the tree and can send his consciousness flying upward to the top in a heartbeat. Sri Chinmoy's last great project, *Seventy-Seven Thousand Service-Trees*, perfectly embodied his direct relationship with the world at large, as he would take the daily moods, doubts and failings of individuals and transform them into a poetic lesson, an illumination with universal application for daily recitation. Here is a sampling:

Insecurity disappears
The moment the light of the soul
Enters into the heart. (No. 4,335)

No more shall I light
A temptation-conflagration
In my aspiration-life. (No. 21,204)

My Lord tells me
Time and again
That I need a special kind of silence
To understand His Whispers. (No. 29,404)

When we bow
To the Supreme in us,
Not only do we melt His Heart,
But also we give Him
A new hope and a new promise. (No. 34,435)

If I do not place myself totally
Inside the Heart of my Lord Supreme
How can I ever claim Him to be
My own, very own? (No. 21,222)

When I start counting my mistakes
God becomes extremely furious.
He says to me: "My child,
Have you nothing else to do?" (No. 38,009)

Each human being
Has to do only one thing:
Unmask his divinity. (No. 36,391)

We can easily live our lives
Without speaking ill of
The rest of the world. (No. 40,031)

God is fully blossomed
In the depths of our hearts,
But our eyes
Fail to see it. (No. 46,205)[35]

Although the style still holds traces of the rhetorical, Sri Chinmoy's tone and the point of view are more modern, direct and aphoristic. The poems command the seeker to step directly into the viewpoint of the poet, the perception from God-heights. Sri Chinmoy explained that a spiritual master must identify with suffering humanity, as well as show the way to the higher point of view. As a student, I felt this ability many times on a personal level, as Sri Chinmoy would sweep the room with his gaze before giving morning prayers. I imagined him plucking the problems, emotions and hidden obstacles from our hearts and minds, before giving them back to us as the day's lessons, amazing us with the

---

35 Sri Chinmoy, *Seventy-Seven Thousand Service-Trees*, series, New York: Agni Press, 2000-07.

expression and appropriation of our own dilemmas. In a talk given in Malaysia, Sri Chinmoy reflected:

> For thousands of things that I have said over the years, I will be sadly, badly misunderstood. There are many, many prayers, countless prayers that I have given in which I use the words "my" and "I". These prayers are not at all applicable to me. I identify myself with other human beings, and then I give the prayers.[36]

Sri Chinmoy has often written interesting commentaries on art, the artist and consciousness. His understanding of inspiration and the Muse also give us an insight from the highest spiritual awareness of the workings of the mind – and as he often explained, although *we* are at the mercy of the Muse, a God-realised soul has the ability to catch and use the Muse at his sweet will. He comments here on the fact that art, poetry, can be a manifestation of a higher level of consciousness:

> When you get a poem from the higher vital world, you will get the feeling of what you call a surge. It is like a very, very big wave, a huge wave, that washes ashore from the ocean. It covers the length and breadth of everything and washes away all impurity and everything else it touches. But when you get a poem from the illumined mental world, even if it just touches you, immediately you feel a sense of illumination in your entire being.[37]

Many of Sri Chinmoy's insights will have far-reaching ramifications both for literary criticism and artistic creation.

---

36 Sri Chinmoy, talk 9 January 2006, Kijal, Malaysia printed in *Beyond Likes and Dislikes*, New York: Agni Press, 2012, p. 74.

37 Sri Chinmoy, *Poetry: My Rainbow-Heart-Dreams*, Germany, 1993, p. 51.

The path that he carved is unique. Far from shunning the physical world, he taught us that we must accept the world for the transformation and the divinization of the world. This path of Sri Chinmoy stands like a lighthouse for humanity, blazing a way forward and encompassing all aspects of the physical world. It is, in fact, a significant new approach to spirituality, which can easily absorb the central truths of all religions while placing the responsibility clearly upon the individual. Sri Chinmoy continually emphasizes that each person must be given complete freedom to find their own path to enlightenment, to the Supreme Consciousness. It is of course the Dream, the ever-transcending Will of the Supreme Consciousness in his Cosmic Game.

> Gazing into the future
> I have come to learn
> That the world will one day
> Succeed in bringing down
> Infinity's Light from Above.[38]

In conclusion, I come back to the original question – why is it so difficult for humanity to hear a new voice? Why has it been so difficult for humanity to understand and utilize the basic truths that the spiritual masters have expressed time and again down through the ages – that the universe is permeated by a higher consciousness and that we are all manifestations of that force?

[38] Sri Chinmoy, *Seventy-seven Thousand Service-Trees*, vol. 31, no. 30,594.

4

Biographical Background of Sri Chinmoy

CHINMOY KUMAR GHOSE was born on 27 August 1931 in the small village of Shakpura, Chittagong in East Bengal (now Bangladesh), the youngest of seven children of Shashi Kumar Ghose (father) and Yogamaya Biswas (mother). Being an energetic child, the youngster was nicknamed Madal, which means "kettledrum". When Madal was still an infant, his eldest brother, Hriday entered the Sri Aurobindo Ashram near Pondicherry, south India. After visiting the *ashram*, it was the fondest wish of Yogamaya that all her children would eventually enter the spiritual life. It was customary for an older brother to give the official name, and it was upon a family visit to the *ashram* that Madal received his proper name of Chinmoy, from Chitta, who wrote in his memoirs:

> In 1936, when we visited the Sri Aurobindo Ashram, the Ashram Secretary, Nolini Kanta Gupta, wanted to know Madal's real name, because Madal is a nickname. I was a little bit puzzled. What suitable name could we give to our youngest brother? Our eldest brother's name is Hriday Ranjan. My name is Chitta Ranjan. My younger brother's name is Manoranjan. Then Prana Ranjan was coming to my mind to give as Madal's real name, but it was not satisfying my heart. All on a sudden, I got an inner message. A divine voice echoed and re-echoed in my heart: "Chinmoy, Chinmoy!" The

3. Sri Chinmoy meditating at Aspiration Ground, New York, circa 1993

meaning of Chinmoy in Sanskrit is "full of divine consciousness".[1]

The young Madal was a creative child and would often sit up in a tree writing poems after his brother taught him Bengali metre. He also loved to go into town with his father and spent long hours observing human nature at the courthouse while his father worked at his Bank. When Madal was eleven years, his father passed away, and, shortly after, his mother Yogamaya also passed away. As a consequence, at the tender age of twelve, Chinmoy joined all his brothers and sisters in entering the Sri Aurobindo Ashram at the end of March 1944, to live under the guardianship of Sri Aurobindo, the great revolutionary and spiritual Master, and the Mother.

On joining the *ashram*, Chinmoy immediately began to have very high inner experiences and became consciously awakened to the spiritual life. He felt an intense inner urge to realise God and would meditate for many hours a day beginning in the small hours before others awoke. By the age of thirteen, he attained a state of enlightenment or Self-Realisation, and would spend many hours in *samadhi* or trance.[2]

The young Chinmoy had no patience with formal schooling, and yet was passionate about learning, studying alone at night. He also took an active part in *ashram* life, especially in the athletic events at which he excelled. For sixteen years consecutively he stood first in the 100 m sprint and was

---

[1] "Chitta's Notebook" in Sri Chinmoy, *My Brother Chitta*.

[2] Sri Chinmoy has recorded the many significant inner experiences he had at this time in his book entitled *Awakening*, Scotland: Citadel Books, 1988.

decathlon champion in 1958 and 1959, his childhood hero being the American sprinter Jesse Owens.[3]

At age fourteen, Chinmoy rendered Sri Aurobindo's Bengali story, "Kshamar Adarsha" (The Ideal of Forgiveness), into Bengali verse – no less than 200 lines of pure Bengali metre. The poet Nirodbaran took it to Sri Aurobindo, who remarked: "It is a fine piece of poetry. He has capacity. Tell him to continue."[4] (The poem was published in a journal, *Partha Sarathi*, in March 1948 with an appreciative editorial note.) By the age of fourteen, Chinmoy had already written 200 poems of his own.

Chinmoy worked in various cottage industries, and took his place doing a share of the daily chores, later saying that washing dishes for hundreds of ashramites gave him the freedom to enter a higher state of awareness. At one stage he translated a work into English by Nolini Kanta Gupta, the General Secretary of the *ashram*, who was so impressed he immediately summoned Chinmoy and appointed him as his own translator and personal secretary.

It was one of the ashramites, Romen Palit, who insisted that Chinmoy should write poems in English and taught him English metre one afternoon. He immediately wrote "The Golden Flute"(published in the ashram journal *Mother India* in October 1953), and over the next few days "Revelation" and

---

[3] Sri Chinmoy eventually had the opportunity to meet the legendary Jesse Owens in America in 1972.

[4] Vidagdha Bennett, *Reverie*.

his classic poem "The Absolute" expressing his most sublime experience of God-realisation.[5]

Chinmoy would have been content to remain in the *ashram* deepening his meditation and taking part in their scholarly activities for the course of his life; however, he explains that an inner Command urged him to travel to the West to share the spiritual knowledge of the East with aspiring seekers in the Western world. After receiving help from sponsors in America, Sri Chinmoy was able to leave India. Thus, on 13 April 1964, at the age of 32, Chinmoy arrived in New York, USA, to a vastly strange new world. Initially, he was able to secure employment as a junior clerk in the Passport and Visa section at the Indian Consulate where he worked for two years.

On arriving in the West, Sri Chinmoy had embarked on giving talks and lectures on the subjects of Hinduism and Eastern spirituality. His first lecture was entitled "Hinduism: The Journey of India's Soul".[6] Over the course of time, seekers became eager to study in depth the teachings and spiritual philosophy of Sri Chinmoy. The first meditation centre was initially called the "Aum" Centre, established in San Juan Puerto Rico in 22 July 1966; followed closely by the second centre in New York. In line with the ancient traditions of *yoga*, Sri Chinmoy was firm in stressing that real spirituality involved purity of mind and body. He taught that the use of drugs was harmful and damaged the subtle spiritual nerves and asked his students to refrain from drugs and alcohol. This was a marked

---

[5] Vidagdha Bennett, *Reverie,* pp. 48ff.

[6] Sri Chinmoy, *My Consulate Years.*

departure from some other practices of the time.

In 1967, with the support of a growing number of disciples, Sri Chinmoy was able to devote himself fully to his spiritual mission. He left his position at the Indian Consulate to devote his time to writing, giving lectures and serving as a guide to his meditation students. From the late 1960s Sri Chinmoy travelled extensively around America and also to Europe and Asia. He offered lectures and public meditations at many universities and colleges. His lectures were on different themes related to spirituality and meditation. During these lecture tours, he also established the first Sri Chinmoy Meditation Centres in Europe and the Far East.

Sri Chinmoy saw inside each individual what he called an aspiration-flame; the quality of aspiration – the heart's ceaseless yearning for ever-higher and deeper realities. He emphasized that this human aspiration was the spiritual force behind all great advances in religion, culture, sports and science. By living in the heart and aspiring for continual self-transcendence, men and women were able to bring forward the best in themselves and find their path to true satisfaction. Indeed, he taught that God Himself is not a static entity, but an ever-transcending level of Consciousness or Being.

Sri Chinmoy has served as spiritual guide to students in some sixty countries around the world, encouraging a balanced lifestyle that incorporates the inner disciplines of prayer and meditation with the dynamism of contemporary life. Sri Chinmoy's own life was an expression of boundless creativity. His vast output spans the domains of musical composition and performance, poetry and literature, painting, sketching, sports and advocacy for peace. His contributions in each of these fields have been striking and far-reaching. The following is a brief summary.

Writings

From an early age Chinmoy was deeply inspired to write books. His first book was *Flame-Waves*, which was published in 1955. Since his first lecture tour in 1968, Sri Chinmoy has spoken at Oxford University, Cambridge University, Harvard University, Dartmouth College, Princeton University, Monash University and many other institutions across the world. His national lecture tour of 1974 took him to a university in each of the fifty states of the US. These fifty talks were later gathered together and published under the title *Fifty Freedom-Boats to One Golden Shore.*[7]

For several years Sri Chinmoy with his disciples published *AUM* magazine, which was dedicated to the publishing of his talks and writings, and became an important early introduction to his philosophy. The first copy of *AUM* was sent to India's president Dr S. Radhakrishnan. He offered generous praise for its spiritual vision and clarity. It is this ability to clarify and expand on ancient philosophies for the modern mind that has become the hallmark of his writings. Since then, Sri Chinmoy's prolific literary output has been printed in over 1,500 books of prose, poetry, plays, stories, questions and answers on the loftiest of themes, as well as memoirs. Most of these books have been published by Agni Press, New York, but other titles have been published by mainstream publishers, including Simon

[7] Sri Chinmoy, *Fifty Freedom-Boats to One Golden Shore.*

& Schuster, Harper and Row, Hazelden, Watkins London, Blue Dove Press California and Health Communications.

Several of Sri Chinmoy's books – the very popular "how-to" guidebook *Meditation* and the more recent *Wings of Joy* and *The Jewels of Happiness* – are international top sellers.[8] Many have been translated into at least fourteen languages. Several libraries and institutions worldwide hold large collections of his published works. Sri Chinmoy's writings constitute a significant contribution to world literature on the subject of spirituality as they contain many references and commentaries on the great spiritual Masters, religions in an evolutionary context and the inner workings of the spiritual life of human beings. One such series is the collection *Sri Chinmoy Answers*.[9] In addition, they reveal unprecedented insights and observations of a spiritual Master who has unbounded access to the secret and sacred worlds of consciousness that, he explains, support and permeate the physical world.

A significant feature of the writings of Sri Chinmoy was the commentary and insight that he brought to bear on topics of modernity, as well as present and past historical figures and movements. He also wrote plays, one on the life of Lord Christ, one on Lord Buddha, on Sri Aurobindo and many on Lord Krishna.[10] The talks and lectures of Sri Chinmoy form much

---

[8] The Jewels of Happiness has now been recorded as an audio-book by many of Sri Chinmoy's prominent friends including Archbishop Desmond Tutu, Carl Lewis, Roberta Flack and Ambassador Awarul Chowdhuri among others.

[9] Sri Chinmoy, *Answers*, vols. 1-38.

[10] *The Son*, *Siddhartha Becomes the Buddha*, *The Descent of the Blue*, and *The Singer of the Eternal Beyond.*

of the basis of his prose works, and his students were still engaged in transcribing and printing these for many years after his passing.

Poetry

When writing poetry Sri Chinmoy often used to say lines of poetry would come to him spontaneously, as if they have already been composed. Like many spiritual poets, Sri Chinmoy's poetry has been described as having a mantric quality. Dr Vidagdha Bennett has described Sri Chinmoy as the seer-poet of our era,[11] and Sri Chinmoy describes the seer-poet as *drashta*, a Sanskrit term for those who have free access to the past, present and future.[12] This is often the thematic reach of his poetry. He has written much about the significance of the twenty-first century in particular, and the new millennium in general, which he projected was the dawning of a new golden age, contradicting the darker view of popular opinion.

The majority of the poetry is written in English. Although Sri Chinmoy felt initially that no other language could capture the ancient sacred tone of the Sanskrit *mantra*, he gradually came to the view that it could be achieved in English. His style ranging from the lyric to prayer and conversation, definition poetry to aphorism and rhetoric, creates a tension between the intimate, personal microcosm and the vastness of the Supreme Consciousness of the Creation.

---

[11] Vigagdha M. Bennett, *Simplicity and Power: The Poetry of Sri Chinmoy*, 1971-81.

[12] Sri Chinmoy, *Poetry, My Rainbow-Heart-Dreams*, p. 12.

Sri Chinmoy was extraordinarily prolific and would set himself challenges in his writings no less than his sporting life. For instance, on a tour of Europe between 21 June 1974 and 13 July 1974 he wrote the volume *1,000 Europe Blossoms*, 100 poems at a time. Other major collections of poetry were *Ten Thousand Flower-Flames*, *Twenty-Seven Thousand Aspiration-Plants* and *Seventy-Seven Thousand Service-Trees* (of which he completed 50,000). There is a clear development in style over the period of these larger collections. In later decades, his major focus was on aphorisms, quite short and primarily intended as a means of spiritual instruction.[13] Sri Chinmoy, who forged his own standards in every sphere of endeavour, also encouraged his students to write, warning them to discard the comments of "the chorus of impossible critics" which unfortunately have the effect of stifling creativity.[14]

Sri Chinmoy at the United Nations

In 1970, under the auspices of the then Secretary-General U Thant, Sri Chinmoy was invited to begin a meditation group at the United Nations. The first meditation meeting was held on 14 April 1970 at the Peace Room of the United Nations Church Centre. Later, on 29 February 1972, Sri Chinmoy had the opportunity to meet U Thant at the United Nations. U Thant said of Sri Chinmoy:

> Whoever speaks to me about you is all appreciation and admiration,

---

[13] The major writings and poetry of Sri Chinmoy mentioned here are available online at: www Sri Chinmoylibrary.com and Sri ChinmoyPoetry.com

[14] Sri Chinmoy, *Poetry, My Rainbow-Heart-Dreams*, p. 14.

> and I personally feel that you have been doing a most significant task for the United Nations. . . . Please feel my sincere respect and sincere concern for what you are doing for mankind.[15]

For thirty-seven years Sri Chinmoy conducted twice-weekly meditation sessions for UN delegates, NGOs and staff members and delivered the monthly Dag Hammarskjold Lecture to further the vision of the UN and promote world harmony. He also served as official representative to the UN for the worldwide Sri Chinmoy Centres, and encouraged many joint projects between them. Sri Chinmoy saw his service to the delegates and staff at the UN as an important step toward bringing forward peace and understanding to the nations of the world. He has written on the future significance of the organization itself.

Sri Chinmoy recognized that the UN was very young in historical terms, but emphasized that it would definitely grow into its highest ideals in the future. He wrote that the UN was not the result of the twentieth century and its conflicts, but the result of the longing for world peace in the heart of humanity from time immemorial, and that although it may take fifty, two hundred, or four hundred years, the dream or vision must eventually be fulfilled even if the outer form changed, again illustrating the importance of aspiration in human development.[16] Many have expressed their profound reverence for his contribution and legacy at the UN. His Excellency Vijay

---

15 Meeting with U Thant, 29 February 1972 at the United Nations headquarters, New York City, recorded in *U Thant, Divinity's Smile Humanity's Cry*, p. 5.

16 Sri Chinmoy, *Inner and Outer Peace*, pp. 48ff.

Nambiar, Under-Secretary-General and UN Chief de Cabinet stated at the UN memorial ceremony for Sri Chinmoy on 30 October 2007, "Sri Chinmoy was far greater than an enlightened individual",[17] yet, unto the end of his life he maintained he was merely a student of peace.

Art

Sri Chinmoy began painting in the mid-1970s – creating a prolific output of spiritually inspirational paintings in a short space of time. Sri Chinmoy calls his artwork "Jharna-Kala", which is Bengali for "fountain-art", he explained, art springing from the source. The name reflects the spontaneous fountain of creativity he experiences through meditation, expressed and revealed through a wide variety of media and forms. He described his technique as a mystical process, a meditation, that he saw a streak of light and simply followed it across the page.

His abstract paintings, which vary from miniature works to huge murals, often would have uplifting themes, representations of a world of light, illustrated with abundant splashes of colour boldly applied using a variety of brushes or sponges. They characteristically flow with a childlike joy, spontaneity and innocence. A number of his paintings form permanent features in galleries and institutions worldwide. The late Raisa Gorbachev, wife of former Soviet Union President Mikhail Gorbachev, was presented with a gift of a large canvas,

---

[17] http://www.srichinmoybio.co.uk/news/celebration-life-sri-chinmoy/

and described Sri Chinmoy's paintings as "a meeting with the nobility of the human soul".[18]

On 16 November 1975 he painted a remarkable 16,031 paintings in one 24 hour period. In the 1990s he took to drawing his distinctive and unique soul birds; rapidly executed pen and ink drawings. These birds have become emblematic of his spiritual artistic works which he terms "Dream-Freedom-Peace-Birds". Sri Chinmoy was particularly fond of the bird motif as he felt it symbolized the ascending human soul seeking to break through the limitations of the physical body. In 2006 the number of Soul-Birds drawn had reached an almost incomprehensible 15 million ranging from the minute collage, through to large Chinese-style banners. These charming and inspiring works have been displayed in art galleries around the world including exhibitions at the UN in New York and the Louvre in Paris, JFK International Airport, UNESCO Paris, London's Mall Galleries and Parliament House, Canberra, Australia.

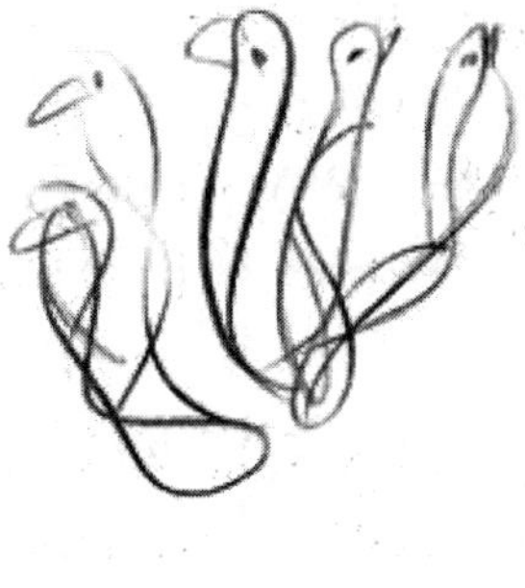

[18] http://nz.srichinmoycentre.org/sri_chinmoy/biography_of_sri_chinmoy/biography_of_sri_chinmoy_3

Some observers look askance at Sri Chinmoy's abundant rate of creation and question the quality of work done so hastily. Sri Chinmoy's reply was that there need not be any conflict between quality and quantity, the "supermarket" of life can be full of abundance. He also explained that his speed of creation came from the fact he sought to use the intuitive, spontaneous capacity of his heart rather than his mind. Sri Chinmoy considered himself to be an instrument of his Supreme Inner Pilot (God) and that his meditation allowed him to become a channel for the divine inner flow of creativity, always present but often dormant.

Sri Chinmoy's Sporting Life

Throughout his life, Sri Chinmoy had been a keen participant in sports. Taking his cue from the *ashram* days, he sought to illustrate how sport could enhance the spiritual life by making the physical a fit receptacle for divine Light. His interest in sport was primarily to compete with oneself, as a form of self-transcendence, yet he did also enjoy and encourage the competitive aspect as a counter to lethargy. He began playing tennis on 13 June 1977, primarily with his students, but occasionally with visiting and professional tennis stars at his own tennis court, later named "Aspiration-Ground", an area large enough for his students to gather for meditation and other activities.

A champion sprinter in his youth, in 1978 at the age of 47, he turned to long distance running and trained hard to complete 22 marathons and 3 ultra-marathons. His fastest marathon time was his first marathon in Chico, California, in which he clocked a time of 3:55:56. Often he would go training as early as 4 a.m. in the morning. Sri Chinmoy wrote numerous accounts of his running experiences in his book series *Run and Become.*[19] He urged his athletic students to train and run marathons, as well as run a 47-mile race that was first staged to mark his 47th birthday, and has been held annually ever since.

Sri Chinmoy founded the Sri Chinmoy Marathon Team (SCMT)[20] which stages a variety of races, from short 2-mile races to triathlons and 24 hour races, some 500 events worldwide, including the world's longest certified race of 3,100 miles held annually in Queens, New York. This event attracts a small following of elite ultra-runners but is largely made up of students of Sri Chinmoy, a testament to the inner and outer strength and endurance of the life of meditation. In many ways the SCMT were a significant pioneer of the rapid growth in ultra-running, which took place in the 1980s. In addition to the 3,100-mile race the SCMT has organized the ultra trio: 700, 1,000 and 1,300 miles. SCMT is recognized for a high standard of organization and for its sensitive support of athletes.

Weightlifting

In the late 1980s, a knee injury curtailed Sri Chinmoy's running career. He advised that his Beloved Inner Pilot then inspired him to take up weightlifting, and so began a new adventure in 1985 at the age of 54 beginning with a 40 pound lift. This was a sport in which previously he had shown little interest, but right from the beginning of his weightlifting career, he was able to make unprecedented progress.

---

19 Sri Chinmoy, *Run and Become*, parts 1-19.

20 www.srichinmoyraces.org/

Specializing in both one-arm lifts and the standing and seated calf-raise, from 1986 Sri Chinmoy performed many unusual lifts and feats of strength with one purpose in mind – to encourage others to believe in and explore their own unlimited potential, in whatever field of life. This was his core belief of "self-transcendence" in action, the capacity of each and every human being to surpass their imagined limitations. Beginning with specially designed overhead apparatus, Sri Chinmoy would sometimes attempt hundreds of times to lift some weights breaking through impossible mental and physical barriers, and eventually built up to the "miracle-lift": an unprecedented 7,063 lb one arm lift (right-arm).

Later, on a custom-built standing calf-raise machine, Sri Chinmoy embarked on demonstration lifts of vast weights, elephants, sailboats, helicopters, Lear jets, grand pianos, trucks and mounted Canadian policemen, to name but a few. The novelty and inspiration he has brought to weightlifting have resulted in enduring friendships with many strength athletes – including the famed Bill Pearl (five times Mr Universe) and Frank Zane – and inspired a renewed interest and understanding of the body–mind, physical–spiritual connection.

In June 1998, Sri Chinmoy founded a unique award programme entitled Lifting Up the World with a Oneness-Heart to honour and celebrate the achievements of people who, in many diverse fields of endeavour, have helped to serve or inspire humanity. Over 8,000 individuals, including Heads of State and Government, Olympic athletes, UN ambassadors and Nobel laureates have received this award. Sri Chinmoy lifted each recipient overhead with one arm on a specially constructed platform. People lifted include Nelson Mandela, Desmond Tutu, Rev. Jesse Jackson, Eddie Murphy, Susan Sarandon, Richard Gere, Yoko Ono, Sting, Carl Lewis, Muhammad Ali, countless other sports stars, Nobel laureates, community leaders, citizens, school-children and politicians.

In September 2006, Sri Chinmoy lifted both Bill Pearl and world champion strongman Hugo Girard at a major bodybuilding competition before an audience of some 1,500 spectators. He claimed:

> If I can inspire someone, and if that person also can inspire me, then we can do many good things for the betterment of this world. Here I am inspiring quite a few people, and they also are inspiring me. If I am inspired, you are inspired and he is inspired, then we shall be able to work together. When we are not inspired, we find fault with other human beings; we quarrel, fight and do many deplorable things. But if we are inspired, then we do many good things for the improvement of this world.[21]

Sri Chinmoy's unorthodox lifting styles sometimes came under criticism for not conforming to the standard forms of weightlifting. Sri Chinmoy's response was thought-provoking, that he was trying to bring newness and vitality into weightlifting in the same way he had done with music, art and running:

> If there is only the dead lift and other standard lifts, then there will be no newness, no invention. Should there be only one game? No,

---

[21] Transcript from an interview with Reuters TV, 4 November 1998, printed in *A Mystic Journey in the Weightlifting World*, part 1, by Sri Chinmoy.

> hundreds of games have been discovered. Then shall we play only football, volleyball and basketball? There should be more games. In a garden will we keep only four types of flowers? If another type of flower appears, we will not cry, "Oh, this is not a flower because for years and years in our garden there have been only four flowers." Unfortunately, when one invents something, it is frequently not accepted. Then a day comes when people forget about the criticism. At first, how much Newton and Einstein suffered! Afterwards, everybody accepted them. In the beginning, newness will always be suspected. It will not be admired and adored. But then, based on that newness, people go forward. . . . If we have to depend on the critics, if we value their opinion, then there will be no newness in this world. Everything will be old, old, old.[22]

In April 2005, Sri Chinmoy's Calf Raise lift was featured in *Muscle and Fitness* magazine as the second most impressive sporting achievement of the year. Up until his *mahasamadhi* (passing), in October 2007, at the age of 76, Sri Chinmoy continued to lift a unique variety of different weights. A film has now been made of Sri Chinmoy's weightlifting prowess entitled "Challenging Impossibility".[23]

Music

During his *ashram* days Sri Chinmoy received a few singing lessons from a music teacher, which helped to train his voice. However, the instruments he played were self-taught; Sri Chinmoy preferred an intuitive approach, which enabled him to compose music from the heart while he was in a state of meditation. He offered over 700

---

[22] Sri Chinmoy, op. cit. http://www.srichinmoylibrary.com/mystic-journey-in-the-weightlifting-world-1/

[23] Found at: www.challengingimpossibility.com/

4. Sri Chinmoy plays the Cello at a Peace Concert, New York, 1996

public concerts ranging up to 19,000 people, in major auditoriums worldwide, always free of charge and usually dedicated to world peace, or to certain individuals whom he felt had contributed greatly to the progress of the world. These included President Gorbachev, President Mandela and Mother Teresa. In 1993, Sri Chinmoy offered 39 concerts in honour of Swami Vivekananda's 39 years on earth, and his momentous attendance at the inaugural World Parliament of Religions in 1893. At his concerts Sri Chinmoy played on a variety of instruments, including traditional musical instruments such as flutes and cellos, as well as percussion and keyboard. His favoured instrument was the north Indian Esraj which he felt most expressive of a spiritual music.

The songs of Sri Chinmoy's are more often meditative and soulful, simple melodies, often with two complementary lines[24] appealing more intuitively rather than intellectually. There are over 21,000 songs in both English and Bengali, primarily mantric and devotional in nature, expressing different aspects of the seeker's spiritual yearning and journey towards the divine. The speed with which he composed both song and melody often had musician scribes scrambling to keep up. Many of the Bengali poems that he wrote as a teenager were later given melodies and turned into songs. Uniquely, Sri Chinmoy has also composed many songs about individuals and individual countries. These songs are also a way of honouring individuals, or highlighting and celebrating the inner

---

[24] Maestro Leonard Bernstein commented: "If I say 'counterpoint' to you, you will ask what that is. But he has written counterpoint like Bach. Every phrase goes with every other phrase, so that no matter what you do, you can't miss. My musical spirit is very, very deeply impressed," in *Sri Chinmoy, The Source of Music*, p. 121.

divine qualities that he observed in people, or in different countries.

> Music is the inner or universal language of God. I do not speak French or German or Italian, but if music is played from any of those countries, immediately the heart of the music enters into my heart.[25]

Sri Chinmoy's compositions, he claimed, came from a high state of meditation to manifest the spirituality or peace of the higher worlds of his experience through music. Likewise, for his performances he entered the meditative state. However, the performances on keyboard instruments, especially piano and organ, were improvisations performed whilst in a meditative state. The experience, designed to draw the listener into the higher state of awareness, would illustrate that it was not all a static state of peace and tranquillity, but could express the divine Power itself. They have been described by many musicians as staggeringly powerful and majestic, yet at the same time, playful and mystical. John Balka, Director of the Office of Sacred Music at St. Mary's Cathedral, San Francisco, observed after hearing a performance of Sri Chinmoy on the pipe organ at St. John the Divine on 15 August 1987:

> Sri Chinmoy has understood that the essence of music has the power to move the soul in ways that words alone cannot. . . . This is how he teaches with music; that is how he moves thousands at a time, through the superconscious, into that perfectly serene light of God's Peace. This is art of the highest order.[26]

---

[25] Music and Meditation at http://www.srichinmoy.org/spirituality/concentration_meditation_contemplation/

[26] Printed in a promotional pamphlet, 1987/88, Sri Chinmoy Centres International.

Work for World Peace

Through various initiatives, Sri Chinmoy sought to illustrate that world peace could only be achieved when people could experience oneness in their consciousness with others through the heart consciousness, rather than through the mind's capacities. He gathered people around him who were receptive to this idea and all his activities were designed to inspire and engender greater understanding and harmony between people. To this end, he met with people from many different walks of life from business people to musicians, sports stars to mountaineers, as well as prominent world leaders, to exchange ideas and offer mutual encouragement. Many became very close friends such as Mikhail Gorbachev and his wife Raisa, and Princess Diana, whom, at her request, he introduced to Mother Theresa in her last years.

One of the most popular initiatives Sri Chinmoy has undertaken, began in 1987 as the Sri Chinmoy Oneness-Home Peace Run,[27] an international torch relay to encircle the globe. This programme has been embraced and expanded into peace studies curricula in schools worldwide and involves many world-class athletes and Olympians, civic and political leaders and thousands of diverse community groups. The Peace Torch has been held by many notable world figures including Pope John Paul II, Mother Teresa, Nelson Mandela, Archbishop Desmond Tutu, Queen Elizabeth II, Dalai Lama, Carl Lewis, Paul and Linda McCartney, Roberta Flack, Jon Bon Jovi, and

[27] www.thepeacerun.org – occasionally known as the World Harmony Run.

the Kings, Presidents or Prime Ministers of many countries. The Peace Torch has been to outer space in the Russian spaceship Mir and been used to light Millennium beacons and the Eternal Flame of Peace at the 50th anniversary celebration of the end of Second World War in Europe.

The stated aim of The Oneness-Home Peace Run is a global relay that seeks to promote international friendship and understanding. As a symbol of peace, runners carry a flaming torch, passing it from hand to hand and heart to heart between hundreds of thousands of members of local communities. The event has visited over 100 nations around the globe. It is organized by an international network of volunteers and Sri Chinmoy's own students, inspired by his vision of a more peaceful world. Sri Chinmoy made the following comment at a function in Sydney on 6 March 1976, which has become the theme of the peace run:

> Right now fear, doubt, anxiety, tension and disharmony are reigning supreme. But there shall come a time when this world of ours will be flooded with peace. Who is going to bring about that radical change? It will be you: you and your sisters and brothers, who are an extension of your reality-existence. It will be you and your oneness-heart, which is spread throughout the length and breadth of the world. Peace is unity. Peace is oneness, within and without.[28]

Another initiative founded by Sri Chinmoy is The Oneness-Heart-Tears and Smiles programme. This humanitarian project has offered and distributed material aid to forty-five countries around the world mainly from donations and superseded or

[28] Sri Chinmoy, *Inner and Outer Peace*, p. 43.

excess goods. Sri Chinmoy explained the aim is to offer more than just financial charity, but to serve humanity with a sense of self-giving.

In 1989 Sri Chinmoy inspired the international Peace-Blossoms programme. This initiative has seen the dedication of some 800 natural wonders, noted landmarks and significant places to world harmony, including Niagara Falls (Canada), the Matterhorn, the Island of Puerto Rico, Gorky Park in Moscow and the Great Barrier Reef in Australia. Each Peace-Blossom is marked by a commemorative plaque and is intended to provide an inspirational focal point for harmony in communities worldwide. Many nations and cities are involved in the Sri Chinmoy Peace-Blossoms programme and support its commitment to nurturing a brighter future for mankind.

In a significant tribute, in both 1993 and 2004 Sri Chinmoy was invited to offer the opening meditation at the Plenary session of the Parliament of the World's Religions, which forms the largest gathering of spiritual and religious leaders and organizations in history. Sri Chinmoy promoted many interfaith activities to encourage religious unity and goodwill – often at the United Nations where he shared his silent non-denominational meditations with the UN leaders, staff members and diplomats each week.

Yoga

The Yoga of Sri Chinmoy is firmly rooted in the spiritual traditions of the Vedas and Upanishads; at the same time, it offers a unique exposition of these ancient ideals, one ideally suited to the Western sensibility. Sri Chinmoy clarified that *yoga* means Oneness, the oneness of all consciousness, and that the physical exercises were preparatory for the reception of a higher consciousness through meditation. Sri Chinmoy's path encompasses all the major paths: of devotion (*bhakti-yoga*), selfless service (*karma-yoga*), meditation (*dhyana-yoga*) and the *yoga* of wisdom (*jnana-yoga*), with the primary objective of the seeker attaining Self-realisation (or God-realisation) through meditation, prayer and discipline. In addition to the inner life, Sri Chinmoy also placed great value on the outer manifestation of inner enlightenment through dynamic dedicated action. He claimed that now was not the time for removing oneself to the Himalayan cave. In his own life, he was a living example of how one can combine the inner life of meditation and prayer with numerous dynamic outer activities.

Despite encompassing these many different aspects, Sri Chinmoy always emphasized that it is the qualities of the heart consciousness, meditating in the heart, which enable the seeker to make the fastest progress. This was juxtaposed against the mind consciousness, which he taught was disposed towards division and supremacy. He felt the heart embodied the ability to identify, and embrace the ideal of oneness. He wrote extensively about the heart consciousness being closer to the divinity of the soul and encouraged seekers to use its intuitive power, as distinct from the mind, which is often bound by its own limitations.

Although a spiritual teacher (*guru*) to many, Sri Chinmoy's teachings emphasize that the only real *guru* is the Lord Supreme. He considered himself to be an instrument of his Beloved Supreme, like an elder brother in the family guiding his younger family members. Another important aspect of Sri Chinmoy's *yoga* is affirmation of the underlying unity of world religions. Frequently he has stated how all religions embody aspects of Truth, and ultimately lead to the same Goal, even if their outer expressions have different emphasis.

Likewise, he taught that each individual must be given complete freedom to find his or her own path towards the Truth. When asked about his own religion, Sri Chinmoy would often state that, although he was raised a Hindu, his only religion was love of God, that there comes a time when one is advanced enough to go beyond religion and commune directly with the Supreme. Nevertheless, his brother Chitta, who lived at the *ashram* for the remainder of his life, observed that the writings of Sri Chinmoy were replete with the ancient Indian Vedic scriptures, reinterpreted for a modern age.

Even in the evening of his life, Sri Chinmoy was remarkably prolific, stating that all of his work, the art, poetry, books, music and other activities were entirely dedicated to the service of aspiring humanity – a "supermarket" of inspiration. He constantly looked for new challenges and new ways to offer inspiration to the world, and claimed that he only needed to sleep two or three hours each night. In addition to his numerous outer activities, Sri Chinmoy, also served as a guide to approximately 7,000 meditation students around the world, and these students, in turn, have been engaged in teaching meditation free of charge to the public in their own countries since the 1970s. He considered the spiritual progress of his students to be one of his most important tasks. Numerous people who had the opportunity to meet and get to know Sri

Chinmoy commented on his untiring selfless dedication to promoting inner and outer peace globally. They also commented on the personal experience of the aura of profound peace, love and joy that he was able to impart while in his presence. He once explained to his students:

> As soon as I come in I bring down Light, Peace and Bliss from above. I bring down a sea of Peace, Light and Bliss, and this moves around like waves of the ocean. . . . I bring down the sea and represent the sea. In that wavy movement. . . . I am actually entering into each disciple. This white Light is the light of purity, inner purity and also it is the consciousness of God in the feminine form; that is to say, it is the Light of the Supreme.[29]

Over 350 Sri Chinmoy Centres now exist in the North and South America, Western, Central and Eastern Europe, Australia/New Zealand, South Africa and Asia. Sri Chinmoy entered the state of *mahasamadhi* on 11 October 2007, aged 76. At the time of his passing, one of the lasting messages from his final year was: "My physical death is not the end of my life – I am an eternal journey." His contribution to the literature and understanding of a higher spiritual consciousness will reverberate through the ages long into the future.

---

[29] Sri Chinmoy, *Perseverence and Aspiration*, p. 62.

Bibliography

Asselineau, Roger, 1980, *The Transcendentalist Constant in American Literature*, New York: New York University Press.

Bennett, Vigagdha M., 1991, *Simplicity and Power: The Poetry of Sri Chinmoy, 1971-1981*, New York: Aum Publications.

———, 2013, *Reverie*, Australia: Equilibrium Books.

Bradbury, M. and J. McFarlane (eds.), 1978, *Modernism: 1890-1930*, Sussex: The Harvester Press.

Champagne, Roland, 1984, *Literary History in the Wake of Roland Barthes*, Alabama: Summa Publications.

Chari, V.K., 1964, *Whitman in the Light of Vedantic Mysticism: An Interpretation*, Lincoln: University Nebraska Press.

Johnson, Thomas H. (ed.), 1961, *Final Harvest: Emily Dickinson's Poems*, Boston: Little Brown & Co.

Kaplan, Justin (ed.), 1982, *Walt Whitman: Complete Poetry and Selected Prose*, New York: Viking Press.

Kher, Inder Nath, 1974, *The Landscape of Absence: Emily Dickinson's Poetry*, Yale: Yale University Press.

Lawrence, D.H., 1951, *Studies in Classic American Literature*, New York: Doubleday & Co.

Levin, S.R., 1969, *Linguistic Structures in Poetry*, Paris/The Hague: Mouton.

Molesworth, Charles, 1983, *Gary Snyder's Vision, Literary Frontiers*, Columbia MO: University of Missouri Press.

Probyn, Clive T., 1984, *English Poetry*, Essex: Longman York Press.

Roberts, J.M. and H. (eds.), 1980, *Selected Poetry of Sri Chinmoy*, New York: Agni Press.

Snyder, Gary, 1957, *Earth House Hold*, New York: New Directions.

———, 1960, *Myths & Texts*, New York: Totem Press.

———, 1967, *Regarding Wave*, Great Britain: Fulcrum Press.

———, 1974, *Turtle Island*, New York: New Directions.

———, 1977, *The Old Ways: Essays*, San Francisco, CA: City Lights Books.

Spense, Alan (ed.), 1982, *Between Nothingness & Eternity: Poems of Sri Chinmoy*, London: Allastree Hill Books.

Dua, Shyam (ed.), 2005, *The Luminous Life of Sri Chinmoy*, Delhi: Tiny Tot Publications.

Sri Chinmoy, 1971, *My Lord's Secrets Revealed*, New York: Herder & Herder.

———, 1972, *My Flute*, New York: Agni Press.

———, 1973, *Commentary on the Bhagavad-Gita: The Song of the Transcendental Soul*, New York: Rudolph Steiner Publications.

———, 1973, *Mother India's Lighthouse: India's Spiritual Leaders,* New York: Rudolph Steiner Publications.

———, 1973, *The Garden of Love Light*, vol. I, Puerto Rico: AUM Press.

———, 1973, *The Heart of a Holy Man: A Book of Spiritual Plays*, New York: Sky Publications.

———, 1974, *Europe-Blossoms*, Puerto Rico: AUM Press.

———, 1974, *Fifty Freedom-Boats to One Golden Shore*, Parts 1-6, New York: Agni Press.

———, 1974, *The Inner Promise: Lectures*, New York: Simon & Shuster.

———, 1974, *Yoga and the Spiritual Life*, New York: Agni Press.

———, 1974, *The Goal Is Won*, New York: Sri Chinmoy Centre.

———, 1974, *The Wings of Light*, New York: Agni Press.

———, 1974, *Samadhi and Siddhi*, New York: Agni Press.

———, 1974, *Selections from The Golden Boat*, New York: Agni Press.

———, 1975, *When God Love Descends*, New York: Agni Press.

———, 1975, *Yesterday I Was a Crying Dream*, New York: Agni Press.

———, 1975, *The Dance of Life*, vol. I, New York: Agni Press.

———, 1975, *Lord, Receive This Little Undying Cry: An Anthology*, New York: Agni Press.

———, 1976, *Perseverence and Aspiration*, New York: Agni Press.

———, 1977, *U Thant, Divinity's Smile Humanity's Cry*, New York: Agni Press.

———, 1978, *Earth's Cry Meets Heaven's Smile*, Puerto Rico: AUM Press.

———, 1979, *Light of the Beyond: Teachings of an Illumined Master*, New York: Agni Press.

———, 1979-96, *Run and Become*, Parts 1-19, New York: Agni Press.

———, 1984, *Inner and Outer Peace*, Montreal: Peace Publishing.

———, 1985, *Meditation: Man-Perfection in God-Satisfaction*, New York: Agni Press, 6th printing.

———, 1988, *Awakening*, Edinburgh, Scotland: Citadel Books.

———, 1990, *The Son*, Edinburgh: Citadel Books.

———, 1991, *Astrology, the Supernatural and the Beyond*, New York: Aum Publications.

———, 1993, *Poetry, My Rainbow-Heart-Dreams*, Augsburg, Germany: Printing Service.

———, 1993, *Siddhartha Becomes the Buddha*, New York: AUM Publications.

———, 1995, *The Source of Music*, New York: AUM Publications.

———, 1995-2002, *Sri Chinmoy Answers*, vols. 1-38, New York: Agni Press.

———, 1996, *My Consulate Years*, New York: Agni Press/Aum Publications.

———, 1997, *The Wings of Joy*, New York: Fireside Simon & Schuster.

———, 1997, *God Is: Selected Writings*, New York: Aum Publications.

———, 1998, *My Brother Chitta*, New York: Aum Publications. Available at http://www.srichinmoylibrary.com/brother-chitta-madal/36.html

———, 1999, *The New Millennium*, New York: Agni Press.

———, 2000, *A Mystic Journey in the Weightlifting World*, Part 1, New York: Agni Press.

———, 2000-07, *Seventy-Seven Thousand Service-Trees*, series, New York: Agni Press.

———, 2002, *The Descent of the Blue*, New York: AUM Publications.

———, 2006, *The Singer of the Eternal Beyond*, New York: AUM Publications.

———, 2010, *The Jewels of Happiness*, London: Watkins Publishing.

———, 2012, *Beyond Likes and Dislikes*, New York: Agni Press.

Steuding, Bob, 1976, *Gary Snyder*, Twayne Publishers, G.K. Hall & Co.

Thoreau, Henry David, 1998, *A Week on the Concord and Merrimack Rivers*, ed. H. Daniel Peck, U.S.: Penguin Books.

Wellek, Rene and Austin Warren, 1942, *Theory of Literature*, San Diego, CA: Harcourt Brace & World.

Weshing, Donald, 1980, *The Chances of Rhyme: Device & Modernity*, Los Angels: University of California Press.

www.srichinmoy.org/library

www.srichinmoyraces.org/

www.challengingimpossibility.com/

www.onenessheart.org/

www.peace.run.org/

www.srichinmoyart.com/

www.srichinmoysongs.com/

www.inspiration-lifts.org/

www.srichinmoypoetry.com/

www.yogaofsrichinmoy.com/

Acknowledgement

The writer acknowledges the biographical notes at:

www.srichinmoy.org

www.nz.srichinmoycentre.org/sri_chinmoy/biography_of_ sri_chinmoy/

www.srichinmoybio.co.uk/srichinmoy

Index